## Voices from the Desert

Leslie Griffiths is a minister in the Methodist Church and a well-known author and broadcaster.

He is a former President of the Methodist Conference and is currently Superintendent Minister of Wesley's Chapel and the Leysian Mission in London.

# Voices from the Desert

*A spirituality for our times*

Leslie Griffiths

*Foreword by*
*Archbishop Rowan Williams*

CANTERBURY
PRESS
Norwich

© Leslie Griffiths 2002

First published in 2002 by the Canterbury Press Norwich
(a publishing imprint of Hymns Ancient & Modern Limited,
a registered charity)
St Mary's Works, St Mary's Plain,
Norwich, Norfolk, NR3 3BH

www.scm-canterburypress.co.uk

Second impression 2003

British Library Cataloguing in Publication data

A catalogue record for this book is available
from the British Library

ISBN 1-85311-491-X

Typeset by Regent Typesetting, London
Printed and bound by
Bookmarque, Croydon, Surrey

I dedicate this book
to the memory
of my brother
Jim (1943–2000)
RIP

# Contents

# Foreword

Leslie Griffiths is one of British Methodism's most distinctive and creative voices: someone whose theology is informed by political and cultural literacy of a rare order, and whose style is direct, engaging and personal without sentimentality. These pages have about them something of the air of a spiritual autobiography; but it is a spiritual autobiography that is also very definitely a history of our times.

The underlying question is how, if at all, the language of the Church becomes credible against the background of various aspects of our age – the violence and racial hatred, the alienation and disillusion of so many, the wasteland of cultural fragmentation. We are introduced to some of the least apparently congenial voices of our cultural environment – the painful anger of American black writing in the sixties, the fiction emerging in the United Kingdom from certain kinds of minority experience, and so on. It does not make for a smooth or obviously edifying conversation; but it presses us to confront the problems of communication across some of the widest and most troubling gaps. Behind much of the text lies a very basic question indeed: how did a faith whose origins had so much to do with life at the margins become so awkward at engaging with the experience of the marginal in the modern period?

It is not just a generational issue, though Leslie Griffiths gives full and appropriate weight to the way in which he – like others – is regularly prodded into reflection by a younger generation. It is to do with how Christians can develop a habit of mind and heart that is sufficiently free from anxiety to engage carefully and gratefully with voices that may not sound easy or welcome. This is a very honest, very stretching, very hopeful book. I trust that it will leave the reader with a sense of the scope not only of the challenge facing Christian language and practice but also of what is already there in that language and practice, waiting to be kindled into life by the gift God gives in the voices of our culture.

Archbishop Rowan Williams

# Preface

I once met Jim Molyneux, at that time leader of the Ulster Unionist Party, at a social function. Suddenly he grabbed my arm, turned his face away from the people in front of us and engaged me in a conversation far more intense than our slight acquaintance seemed to warrant. I did my best to oblige. A moment or two later, thanking me profusely, he explained himself. It seems that he'd seen Ian Paisley ambling towards us and, for some reason related to the intricacies of Irish politics at that time, didn't under any circumstances want to become a fellow either hailed or well met by the leader of the Democratic Unionists. 'That man,' said Mr Molyneux, 'has never approved anything in his life. He's perfected a thousand ways of saying NO.'

There is a sense in which Dr Paisley displays the instincts of the Christian Church. It so often tends to be reactive. It assumes that the world is wicked and turns away from it. It finds a thousand ways to say no to the innovative or the pleasurable. It defines itself *contra mundum*, over against the world. At times it buttresses its position by an appeal to some form of dualism that separates the here and now from some mystical hereafter and whose roots lie much more in the thinking of Plato than Christ. Or else it justifies itself by appealing to precedent and, to this end, expects its theologians to write about (or from within) 'the tradition' and its bishops to do or say nothing of any consequence without first consulting their canon lawyers.

I caricature, of course, but only to make a point. Too often the Church has been dismissive of the culture that surrounds it, fearing it for its pagan or its blasphemous, its risky or its heretical content. There may, sometimes, be an element of truth in such thinking. Often, however, the efforts of creative people to engage seriously with matters of life and death, meaning and value, epistemology and apologetics, spirituality and even theology, are pushed away in favour of the dominating voices whose 'thus saith the Church' evokes a distant and ironic echo of the prophet's 'thus saith the Lord'.

I have done my share of this, reading only what belonged to the tradition or what I was comfortable with. I've been ready to form 'attitudes' about subjects I had scarcely any knowledge of, based often enough on little other than my feelings or even prejudices. In common with others, I steered clear of a great deal that belonged to popular culture suspicious of its syncretisms or its imaginative leaps, its tackiness or its irreverence. Until, that is, I found myself put firmly on the spot by the people who never flinch from telling it 'how it is'. My family.

One Sunday, we were all sitting at table expansively after a good lunch. That morning, I'd preached a sermon I was very pleased with. I'd expected some comment over the meal or even, indeed, a compliment or two. But nothing came. So, the last refuge of the ignoble mind, I tried to provoke them into saying something. An uncomfortable silence was broken by one of our children who, damning my sermon with the barest trace of praise, went on to inform me that my rather erudite pulpit efforts seemed only rarely to focus on the world in which young people lived or the pressures they lived under.

This observation shook me to the quick. After a routine denial, I retreated to my study to sulk. I looked along my bookshelves and, oh dear, saw such a dreary and predictable library. And then I cast an eye over our collection of music. How very, very conventional. So I began to launch out a bit. I'd always read novels but now deliberately sought out those written from other cultures. Naipaul, Oz, Mahfouz, Lovelace, Kundera, Marquez – I devoured them all. Why hadn't I done this before? I widened my musical interests too but, while I never came to like much pop music or rock 'n' roll, I did become more aware of what it was all about. I certainly came to realize how important it is, a key even, for any understanding we may form of our contemporary culture.

I began, very tentatively, to share some of the things I was becoming aware of with individuals and audiences of various kinds. They helped me greatly with their comments, not all of them complimentary. I don't think I've got near the bottom of things but I'm certainly much more alert to a world within which there's a great deal of anger and alienation. It's also a world where there's a deep spiritual yearning, a need for something to hang on to, a search for enlightenment and meaning.

Has there ever been a time when the institutional Church was so rejected? It's perceived as being out of touch, moralistic, weird even. Much of the criticism it receives is wide of the mark but, as some wise old bird keeps saying these days, it's the perception that counts. One of the things that the Church must do better is listen. It does, after all, believe in a God who, according to the Bible, himself listened to the groans of his people again and again when they were in trouble. I've done my best on this score and this little book represents my attempt to make out what some of the voices of our own day are saying. These are voices from the desert, the voices of people who've often been dismissed or rejected by the Church and who, in their turn, have been happy enough to return the compliment. I think I understand some of the things they're saying a little better now than I used to, but there's lots more listening to do.

Jack Kerouac dominates the first chapter. The Beat Generation seem to me to have laid the foundation for a whole post-war culture with their openness to new experience and their determination to live the present moment to the full. Their ready use of drugs and alcohol, their unrestrained sexual experimentation, challenged conventional lifestyles and the traditional teaching of the Church. They were roundly condemned for their pains. I've brought Dietrich Bonhoeffer into the same chapter as Kerouac and his friends, suggesting that he, like them, was on a road. His search too was for freedom.

This takes us naturally into the second chapter, which looks at the 1960s. The social revolution associated with that decade offered people new freedoms and opportunities. It also produced its own reaction and stirred many people up to question the kind of society we were becoming. Andy Warhol, George Harrison, Eldridge Cleaver, Martin Luther King and Maya Angelou are examined here, an admittedly eclectic group but who seem in various ways to respond to the spirit of the times in interesting and important ways.

The next two chapters are somewhat different. The first (Chapter 3) takes a long, hard look at Wales. The collapse of non-conformity has left a vacuum in the spiritual life of the nation and some unusual voices are being raised to fill it. Among these are the searing lyrics and angry music of The Manic Street Preachers and the bleak novels of Niall Griffiths. But no one looked into the soul of Wales more poignantly than the Christian poet R. S. Thomas. In Chapter 4, I've tried to examine the recent history of Haiti. Here I must ask my readers to be patient with me. A somewhat detailed overview of Haitian history is intended to show the plight not only of that hapless nation but the situation in which many poor countries find themselves. I've tried to say a good word for a dictator and to show how liberation theology was a theological response to the same social factors that he tried to face politically.

The final chapter moves beyond particular countries and into a post-colonial world and the literature of displaced people. Many familiar landmarks have been swept away and things and people lose their rootedness. Everything displays a more hybrid nature, old distinctions have disappeared. Salman Rushdie and Hanif Kureishi seem to embody these factors and I take a look at some of their work before ending with an examination of Hans Küng's treatment of the nature of Christian identity.

When someone comes to explore a new and rich area of experience somewhat later in life than might have been the case, it's inevitable that there'll be something eclectic about the choices he makes, and I'm perfectly aware that that's true of mine. For all that, I offer them in the belief that they all say something important and deserve to be heard.

In each chapter I've tried to imagine a theological voice, someone from the world of belief, who seemed to be wrestling with the same themes as those in the popular culture of their time. Usually, and regrettably, the two worlds rarely met. Nor do they, for the most part, even now. If they did, and I've come to feel this more and more strongly, it could be such fun. There'd be sparks flying for a while, all kinds of mutual misunderstandings would have to be cleared up and, when all that had happened, we could all get on with the business of enjoying each other. We could have such a party and take so much pleasure in each other as we discovered each other as if for the first time. That's the dream that I've formed by listening to these voices that often come from some very bleak places and from some pretty dark experiences. Yet they've always had something real and challenging to say. And, for what they are, I'm glad to share them now with a wider audience through the pages of this book.

Leslie Griffiths
May 2002

# Down on the rocks: the Beat Generation

My daughter's graduation gave me one of the thrills of my life. She had studied at the same university and in the same faculty as I had. So, when she came to walk across the stage to collect her diploma, she wore the same hood and mortar board as I had 30 years previously. Wonderful. But this was by no means the only pleasure my daughter's higher education afforded me. Whereas my two sons had gone off into fields of learning that I knew much less about, my daughter had chosen to study modern languages and literature and that gave us lots of shared pleasure.

Apart from the set texts and the official booklist that preoccupied her for much of her time, I took special interest in what I can only call 'campus literature', books that students of all disciplines seemed to have on their shelves. There were, of course, items that hadn't even been written when I was a student, works like Pirsig's *Zen and the Art of Motorcycle Maintenance* and Peck's *The Road Less Travelled*. But there were two hardy perennials there to be seen, works that had been widely read and discussed in my time too. Someone, sometime, needs to work out the influence of Nietzsche in general and *Thus Spoke Zarathustra* in particular on succeeding generations of developing minds. The lucid prose and the winsome arguments of this brilliant piece have been devoured by so many of our young and thinking people. It's a work which asks how the shadow of God can be obliterated, how traces of his presence can be effaced, and how all consequences of belief in God can be eliminated. It argues that it's only when man rises above himself that he can enter into a 'higher history' and become equal to the gods. It goes on to talk of the superman (the man who succeeds in overcoming man) who inhabits earth not heaven, here and not hereafter and who, after God's death, takes God's place. The other major theme developed in this book is the eternal recurrence of the same: we shall have to live all our experiences and feelings all over again. This 'ring of recurrence' constitutes Nietzsche's understanding of eternity.

The other book Ruth and I had in common was Jack Kerouac's *On the Road*. I believe this to be a seminal work that shaped a whole culture in the years following the Second World War. Kerouac himself had devoured the writings of Nietzsche. The sheer energy and the rootlessness of his classic novel, its description of lifestyles (and worldviews) based on experience, pleasure, drug-induced mind expansion, sexual experimentation and a freedom from prevailing conventions gave it an immediate place in the best-selling lists. And it brought the word 'beat' into common currency.

Kerouac was born in 1922 in Lowell, a small textile town 30 miles north of Boston. His family's origins were in Brittany and strongly Catholic. He grew up speaking French and his childhood was marked by the death of his older brother Gerard and a regular round of religious observances in a church dominated by images of a suffering or dying Christ. He gained a reputation at field sports – football, baseball and athletics. At home, he observed his mother carefully, the way she idealized her lost son, and put up with a husband who drank heavily and lost money on cards. He noticed too the comfort afforded her by her religion. His father was forced out of his business by a natural disaster and, without insurance, saw the loss of all his assets. He became disenchanted with the American dream and talked repeatedly of the time when 'America was America, when people pulled together and made no bones about it'. Jack Kerouac had a voracious love of literature and that, together with his outstanding sporting ability, led him to New York and Columbia University.

Half of Kerouac's novels are set in Lowell and it was there he spent his last years before he drank himself to death in 1969. But it was New York that exposed him to a pace of life and a group of people who would change the direction and affect the tone of everything he did. This very American boy soon abandoned his formal studies; he spent a desultory time in the armed forces; he gave up his interest in sport. He was drawn into a circle of friends whose promiscuous lifestyle, use of drugs, love of jazz and association with criminals, pushers and the psychiatrically disturbed led him into a world well beyond the limits and conventions of his upbringing. He had found the raw material for his writing.

Allen Ginsberg was one of this group of friends. Born in 1926, he was raised in Paterson, New Jersey, the son of a schoolteacher father who wrote poetry and a mother suffering from paranoid schizophrenia. Both his parents, of Russian Jewish immigrant stock, had strong socialist views. Indeed, his mother was a member of the communist party and wanted her son to gain the qualifications needed to become a labour lawyer and help working-class Americans. Soon after arriving at Columbia, he met Jack Kerouac and they immediately became friends. Ginsberg was a homosexual. Like his mother, he spent long periods within psychiatric institutions. He saw apparitions and suffered periods of intense depression. He soon realized that poetry rather than law was to be the business of his life.

The third member of this group was William Burroughs. He was a few years older than the others and hailed from St Louis, Missouri. Among his antecedents were Methodist preachers and Yankee entrepreneurs. His grandfather had invented and marketed the adding machine. He became fully aware of his homosexual orientation from a very early age. He studied English at Harvard and found it extremely dull. St Louis was duller still despite one or two love affairs. He eventually headed for New York and had soon made the acquaintance not only of writers and musicians in lower Manhattan but also of petty criminals who clearly fascinated him. He was soon heavily dependent on drugs and wildly promiscuous in his sexual practice. He was widely read and set about shaping the reading patterns of Kerouac and Ginsberg, to say nothing of their lifestyles. He wrote only fitfully at first but the trickle of novels he published were all to prove highly controversial.

Burroughs moved in with Joan Adams in the mid-1940s. Like him, she was heavily dependent on benzedrine. The relationship ended in Mexico with a bizarre event. While both of them were in a drugged stupour, he attempted to shoot at an apple placed on her head (his 'William Tell' act, as he called it). He missed the apple and the bullet passed through Joan's head and she died instantly. This was to affect Burroughs for the rest of his life.

Kerouac, Ginsberg and Burroughs were the key members of a much larger group that collectively became known as 'the Beat Generation'. The word 'beat' has two meanings. The first connotes beaten down or exhausted. 'Man, I'm beat' meant that someone was tired, done in, weighed down. Simple enough. But Kerouac took it to express the feeling of all those people he identified with who'd been knocked down and relegated to the margins of society. It was the feeling that linked the poor blacks of Virginia with the junkies, queers and madmen he met in New York. 'To me,' said Kerouac, 'it meant being poor – like sleeping in subways and yet being illuminated and having ideas about apocalypse and all that.'

This identification with society's cast-offs was to become a key to Beat writing. Broadly speaking, Jack Kerouac was intrigued by hobos and the racially stigmatized, while Allen Ginsberg became interested in sexual outlaws and William Burroughs in criminals and drug addicts. This was partly because they saw these social groups as having rejected (and been rejected by) mainstream America, and partly because they believed that a new vision of life would only emerge once the veneer of 'civilized values' had been stripped away.

The identification with society's rejects, or at least with those who lived on or beyond the margins of conventional society, resonated with ideas being explored by Michel Foucault (1927–84). Central to Foucault's thinking is the Nietzschean idea of 'the limit experience', an experience that transforms the self – one's way of thinking, one's assumptions and beliefs – by going beyond the bounds of normality. He was always aiming to unsettle what he identified as universally held values by digging beneath them and, in particular, he searched out people who challenged such values and thus provoked their reinforcement, the people who dared to go (in Nietzsche's phrase) 'beyond good and evil' – the mad, the criminals and the perverts. Foucault applied this thinking to his own life, he explored the values that shape us all by attempting to discover their limits, by himself going into the realm beyond good and evil. The inner logic of his philosophical odyssey is 'unintelligible apart from his lifelong, and highly problematic, pre-occupation with limiting the limits of reason, and finding ways – in dreaming, at moments of madness, through drug use, in erotic rapture, in great transports of rage, and also through intense suffering – of exploring the most shattering kinds of experience'.[1]

At this time, too, the insights of what was to become known as 'liberation theology' were pushing the Roman Catholic Church through a series of hoops that were to result in the famous axiom that the Church should always be exercising 'a preferential option for the poor'. We'll be looking at that in Chapter 4 but it needs noting here.

The Beat Generation became preoccupied with these ostracized people from the outset and could, arguably, be shown to have set the scene and established the agenda for philosophers and theologians alike for a couple of genera-tions.

The Christian doctrine of original sin, which had in-spired so many of the traditional values of America, was tipped on its head by these writers. In Christian thinking, humans were tainted by 'original sin' and needed the 'common grace' of civilization to restrain them and the 'special grace' of Christ to save them. In Beat thinking, humans were essentially 'holy' beings who had been cor-rupted by civilization and could be saved by rediscovering their original natures.[2]

It was the poor who were Beat (beaten down) and yet, as Kerouac added, they were 'illuminated' too. This second level of meaning emerged from the first. The word 'beat' was linked to the word 'beatific' and its associates. 'Blessed are the poor, the sorrowful, those of a gentle spirit,' Jesus had said. The Beatitudes bring centre stage the same people identified by the Beats. So the poor and the oppressed, the marginalized and the unwanted, were included within the ambit of Beat life, and they were to be understood as people of value, people with character, interesting people. This was 'a Catholic beatific vision, the direct knowledge of God enjoyed by the blessed in heaven'.[3]

*On the Road*, begun in the immediate post-war years but not published until 1957, sets the tone for all this. It's the story of Dean Moriarty, 'traveller and mystic, the living epitome of Beat'. Kerouac had begun by envisioning his work as a quest novel like Cervantes' *Don Quixote* or John Bunyan's *Pilgrim's Progress*, but it soon acquired its own characteristics. It set out 'to test the American dream by trying to pin down its promise of unlimited freedom'.[4] As Dean explains to the narrator Sal Paradise:

> 'You spend a whole life of non-interference with the wishes of others . . . and nobody bothers you and you cut along and make it your own way . . . What your road, man? – holyboy road, madman road, rainbow road, guppy road, any road. It's an anywhere road for anybody anyhow. Where body how?'

And Dean throws himself into his journey across America in search of this paradisal experience of freedom at an exhilarating non-stop pace that makes even the reader breathless. He stands out among Sal Paradise's other friends, all of them intellectuals, like a shining light. The others include those described as a 'Nietzschean anthropologist', a 'nutty surrealist' and a critical nihilist. Dean, on the other hand, had

> intelligence [that] was every bit as formal and shining and complete without the tedious intellectualness. And his 'criminality' was not something that sulked and sneered, it was a wild yea-saying overburst of American

joy; it was Western, the west wind, an ode from the Plains, something new, long prophesied, long a-coming (he only stole cars for joy rides). Besides, all my New York friends were in the negative, nightmare position of putting down society and giving their tired bookish or political or psychoanalytical reasons, but Dean just raced in society, eager for bread and love; he didn't care one way or the other, 'so long's I can get that lil ole gal with that lil sumpin down there tween her legs, boy,' and 'so long's we can *eat*, son, y'er me? I'm *hungry*, I'm *starving*, let's *eat right now*!' – and off we'd rush to *eat*, whereof, as saith Ecclesiastes, 'It is your portion under the sun.'[5]

The whole book glints with literary references, all those writers who left their mark on Kerouac but also shaped modern sensibilities. Goethe, Dostoyevsky, Nietzsche, Spengler, the Marquis de Sade, Kafka, Celine, Alain-Fournier and Hemingway. But it's jazz that really sets Dean's (and Kerouac's) heart on fire. Jazz sessions give Dean his best times on the road, symbolizing the source of American freedom and creativity.

Jazz and bebop were musical styles that were beginning to emerge from the culture of black America and cross over into white culture. *On the Road* has a number of graphic descriptions of musical experiences.

Take jazz pianist George Shearing, for example, who fingers his keyboard gently at first, bringing a rippling sound from it; his bass-player leans reverently towards him, merely thrumming the beat, while the drummer is described as barely moving. Then the tempo picks up until Shearing begins to rock; smiles break out on previously passionless faces, the language begins to describe ecstasy. The beat goes up even more, bodily movement increases, all three musicians change gear. Members of the audience become participators: 'Go,' they shout. 'Old God Shearing', proclaims Dean Moriarty who's gone into convulsions of ecstasy. And when the old musician finally leaves the piano stool, after a session intense with passion and triumphant with rapture, Dean, pointing to where the maestro has been sitting, announces 'God's empty chair.' The narrator adds his own laconic comment. 'This', he says, 'is the moment when you know all and everything is decided forever.'[6] The whole incident, set in a New York bar, bristles with religious meaning and association.

A similar atmosphere is conveyed with brilliant effect by the description of an evening in a San Francisco bar.[7] Kerouac lays bare the total commitment of the musicians to their art and somehow reveals the depth within them from which their sound comes. He also portrays the synergy between instrumentalists and audience, the sheer empathy and association that binds them to each other. And the song is always the song of love: 'Make it dreamy for dancing, while we go romancing. Love's holiday will make it seem okay. So baby come just close your pretty little eyes.' The rapture, the swooping of the trumpet, the holding of notes and the exploration of rhythm, make the whole musical exercise seem like a quest, a search within oneself, an agonizing, a discovering, an expressing, a triumphant outburst before ending in collapse and a sense of disgust with 'ordinary' life. The pattern of this musical moment seems to image both the essence of lovemaking and the rapture of religious experience. They all seem dug from the same quarry; they somehow connect the human psyche to the same elemental energies, to allow the practitioner to transcend sense experience and everyday events in a way that links him or her to the source of life itself. Ecstasy, orgasm, the very pitch of pathos, the yea-saying overburst of joy, are all in the music, the lovemaking, the sense of the numinous. 'My God I am thine, what a comfort divine, what a blessing to know that my Jesus is mine. In the heavenly lamb, thrice happy I am, and my heart it doth dance at the sound of his name.' Who knows whether this verse of a hymn, written by Charles Wesley still in the grip of his conversion experience, isn't made of the same raw material?

Much of this experience within Kerouac's novel was the result of alcohol- or benzedrine-induced states of mind. Somehow the doors of perception were opened, inhibitions disappeared, life lay waiting to be seized. Sex, music and roaming the wide open spaces became ways of expressing those inner freedoms half-seen in moments of rapture and ecstasy. But there was often a price to pay. Kerouac himself paid it. He drank himself to death at an early age. But it was Allen Ginsberg who showed the truly horrendous shadow side of all the upbeat, racy, life-grabbing approach to life demonstrated by Dean Moriarty and his associates – nowhere is this more forcefully described than in the poem 'Howl'.

This poem was dedicated to the memory of Carl Solomon, one of the close circle of friends that clung to Burroughs, Ginsberg and Kerouac. Ginsberg had met him in a psychiatric institute where he'd spent long periods of time. Seeing his plight had distressed Ginsberg enormously. So too had the death of Joan Burroughs in 1951. The poem is filled with agony and surrealist, apocalyptic visions that themselves seem the product of a mind that's been opened up by drugs. It rails against the way things are and mourns the loss or the destruction to be seen on all hands. Its opening sets the tone for the rest of the poem:

I saw the best minds of my generation destroyed by madness, starving hysterical naked,

dragging themselves through the negro streets at dawn
    looking for an angry fix,
angelheaded hipsters burning for the ancient heavenly
    connection to the starry dynamo in the machinery of
    night,
who poverty and tatters and hollow-eyed and high sat up
    smoking in the supernatural darkness of cold-water
    flats floating across the tops of cities contemplating
    jazz . . .[8]

and so on. In his breathless list of some of the casualties of
the contemporary world, Ginsberg makes reference to
communism, drugs and, of course, sex. He writes of those
who've endured waking nightmares, those who though
intelligent shake with shame, those who've gone 'yacketay-
yakking screaming vomiting whispering facts and memories and anecdotes and eyeball kicks and shocks of hospitals
and jails and wars', or those whose sexual activities have
left them empty, disillusioned, crashed out. There's a sense
in which the poem is one, long, lurid catalogue of woe. Its
overt references to copulation, masturbation and sexual
experimentation suggest the obsessions and fetishes of the
author and they make sad reading. The scenes and the
states of mind being described seem so pointless and bale-
ful. One easy response to such self-indulgence is to dismiss
it on the grounds that this is clearly the work of an alienated, dysfunctional and somewhat pathetic man. Its author
seems to be lashing out with no obvious focus for his anger.
At least not in the first 78 long (sometimes very, very long)
lines of this poem.

But there has to be more to it than that. Ginsberg became
iconic for many people of his generation. To them, he
seemed to be identifying a social malaise (and a response to
it) that was palpable. It's in the second part of the poem

that the object of his (and his generation's) disillusion becomes clearer. Still mourning the senseless loss of Carl Solomon and others, his questions rain down a string of accusations. The opening line sets up everything that follows. Referring still to all the 'best minds' so senselessly destroyed, the poet asks with some insistence:

> What sphinx of cement and aluminum bashed open their skulls and ate up their brains and imagination?[9]

The answer to his question, and subsequent object of his wrath, the one who causes such senseless death and the descent into madness, is identified as 'Moloch'. In a set of nine maledictions, Moloch, the child-devouring god of ancient times, is blamed for all kinds of social ills. He it is who brings sorrow to young men conscripted into the army and old men weeping in the parks. Moloch is named as 'the Congress of sorrows', whose mind is 'pure machinery', whose blood is 'running money', whose fingers are 'ten armies', whose breast is a 'cannibal dynamo'. This is the god of impassive skyscrapers, satanic factories, banks, urban pollution, weapons of mass destruction, robot apartments, the god from whom there is no escape except, perhaps, that afforded by drugs. Visions, miracles and ecstasies have 'gone down the American river'. The only way to break free from Moloch's grip is somehow to break out and cross this river.

> Highs! Epiphanies! Despairs! Ten year animal screams and suicides! Minds! New loves! Mad generation! down on the rocks of Time!
> Real holy laughter in the river! They saw it all! The wild eyes! The holy yells! They bade farewell! They jumped off the roof! To solitude! Waving! Carrying flowers! Down to the river! Into the Street![10]

It is the whole capitalist, industrial, military machine that Ginsberg is lashing out at while railing at the symbols of bourgeois aspirations and lifestyles that he considers so unremittingly soul-crushing.

It is not difficult to see why, when 'Howl' was finally published in 1957 it was seized by the police and application made to the courts that it be judged obscene and withheld from circulation. Eventually, judgement came down in favour of the poem to the great delight of Ginsberg and his friends. Even so, they were very nervous about some of the detail in the poem that allowed an all too easy identification of various individuals and spread out for public view the activities of the Beats. And the fuss surrounding the case, together with the elation following its successful outcome, allowed public attention to focus on the fevered, almost Old Testament, prophetic scream of opposition to the spirit of the age. Less recognized than the impact of this drug and sex-dominated poem, however, yet a similar attempt to escape from the mechanized modern world, was Ginsberg's 'discovery' of Buddhism and the sustained attempt he made to find inner peace through its teachings.

It was a San Francisco poet Gary Snyder who stimulated and developed Ginsberg's interest in Buddhism. Snyder had a degree in oriental languages from Berkeley and was a serious student of Zen. He was also a very practical man whose simple lifestyle was lived in the outback. Ginsberg and Kerouac had already shown a superficial interest in Eastern religion. Ginsberg didn't make too many claims for this freshly discovered source of spiritual enlightenment, however. He was sufficiently open-eyed to recognize that there was little crossover between his own dissolute way of life and the simplicity and asceticism of the Buddhists but he found himself captivated by a painting of Sakyamuni (one of the Buddhas) coming down from his mountain hermitage, so much so that he penned a short poem about it as an immediate response to the qualities he saw within it.

> He drags his bare feet
>> out of a cave
> in ragged soft robes
>> wearing a fine beard
>> unhappy hands
> clasped to his naked breast –
>> humility is beatness.

As one commentator puts it: 'emerging from his mountain-side cave, the beat Buddha appeared to be an icon of self-sufficiency, spiritually fortified against money, worries, parent pressure and sex that crazed the mind'.[11]

While Ginsberg drew back from any more full-blooded exploration of Buddhist spirituality, Kerouac seemed poised to embrace Eastern religion with far more commit-ment. He discovered and devoured Henry David Thoreau's *Walden*, a work composed as long ago as 1845. Thoreau had constructed a rough hut on the shore of Walden Pond near Concord, Massachusetts, in a deliberate attempt to turn his back on the traditional Puritan values of hard work and profit. Instead, he turned to the rigours of contempla-tion. He sought to become less a cog in a machine, more a particle of the universe. As Campbell puts it: '*Walden* became the ur-text of Beat Buddhism: practical in its back-woodsmanship, sound in its ecological principle, and useful as a guide to the classic Hindu texts.'[12] Kerouac went on to study Ashvagosa's *Life of Buddha*, Dwight Godard's *A Buddhist Bible* and *The Gospel of Buddha* by Paul Carus before writing up his impressions and reflections at some length. Then he read the *Sutras*, texts that are thought to transmit the words of Buddha himself. 'If you are now desirous of more perfectly understanding Supreme Enlightenment and the more enlightening nature of pure Mind-Essence, you must learn to answer questions spontaneously with no recourse to discriminating thinking,' the Buddha had said. This pleased Kerouac who applied the notion 'first thought, best thought' to all his subsequent writing. From that time on, he avoided editing or modifying his writing and criticized others who seemed ready to do so.

For ten years, Kerouac took Buddhism seriously. It seemed to offer solutions to his feelings of alienation and his terror of death. Buddhism teaches that such sorrow comes from our failure to let go of illusions. We suffer because of 'ignorant desire'. We feel lonely because we fail to accept that life is only a dream anyway. The moment it dawns on us that nothing is real, we loosen our grip and are rewarded with joy. Kerouac gave himself seriously to the meditative techniques that would bring his mind into such an experience of enlightenment.

Indeed, he wanted to gain this inner solace so badly that, following the example of Gary Snyder, in June 1956 he worked as a lookout on Desolation Peak in the Mount Baker National Forest. He spent 63 days there in the hope that his isolation from human company would afford him ample opportunity to meditate and come face-to-face with God (or the void) and 'find out once and for all what is the meaning of all this existence and suffering and going to and fro in vain'. But he ended this time desperate for company and kicks.

So Kerouac, like Ginsberg, found he lacked the stamina and will power fully to enter the Buddhist discipline. For all that, with organized Christianity (in its Catholic and Protestant forms) thought to be inextricably bound up with the American military-industrial complex, the Beats established a trend away from formal religious observance and towards 'inner development', away from the search for truth and towards feelings. In Buddhism, there was no need to believe in God, the ten commandments, heaven, hell or even the existence of an afterlife. Buddhism offered a clean image; it couldn't be blamed for creating the dark side of modern Western civilization. Its message was peacefulness, harmony with nature and non-attachment to material goods. Its leaders were not men in suits and ties who fronted multi-million-dollar religious organizations but were monks in saffron robes who practised a simple lifestyle and condemned no one. And Buddhism stood miles apart from 'Christian' America, which had dropped its atom bombs on Hiroshima and Nagasaki.

Despite all this deep mystical yearning for a spirituality free from all association with the darker side of Western values and lifestyles, there was something within Buddhism that didn't quite command either respect or total commitment from any of the Beats. Of all people, it was William Burroughs who made the most pointed observation on this matter when he wrote to Kerouac as follows:

Remember, Jack, I studied and practised Buddhism (in my usual sloppy way to be sure). The conclusion I arrived at, and I make no claims to speak from a state of enlightenment, but merely to have attempted the journey . . . Was that Buddhism is only for the West to *study as history;* that is, it is a subject for *understanding*, and yoga can profitably be practised to that end. But it is not, for the West, *An Answer*, not *A Solution*. We must learn by acting, experiencing, and living: that is, above all, by *Love* and by *Suffering* . . . You were given the power to love in order to use it, no matter what pain it may cause you. Buddhism frequently amounts to a form of psychic junk . . . What I mean is the Californian Buddhists are trying to sit on the sidelines and there are no sidelines. Whether you like it or not, you are committed to the human endeavour.[13]

Kerouac took this observation with the utmost seriousness. Indeed, he had even dared to take a critical look at the freedoms and joyousness so powerfully expressed in *On the Road*. He knew that while the book's action might well centre on joy, the scaffolding holding it in place was despair. 'Where go? What do? What for?' In its own way the book is an effort to describe a life of not-thinking – but without a spiritual dimension. Kerouac had fought back against the darkness of his despair with kicks in the form of sex, benzedrine, liquor, travel, and a big fix of words. But the despair, which brought an overwhelming sense of purposelessness, finally got him.

Dietrich Bonhoeffer might seem a strange person to introduce at this stage. Yet his book *The Cost of Discipleship* created quite a stir through the very years when Kerouac and Ginsberg were making their own impact. An abridged version appeared in English in 1948 and the first complete edition nine years later. Much of the book consisted of an extended commentary on the Sermon on the Mount, the classic utterance of a first-century wandering prophet who was himself constantly 'on the road'. The sermon opens, of course, with (what else?) the Beatitudes. In his exposition of these, it's clear that Bonhoeffer understood Jesus to be coupling precisely the two meanings of the word 'beat' that Kerouac and his friends favoured. The disciples of Jesus, by renouncing everything they had to follow him, 'are living in want and privation, the poorest of the poor, the sorest afflicted, and the hungriest of the hungry'.[14] These beat-up men could, therefore, identify with all the down-beaten people who crowded around

Jesus and who hung on his every word. Bonhoeffer distinguishes these marginalized and powerless people from 'the
representatives and preachers of the national religion, who
enjoy greatness and renown, whose feet are firmly planted
on the earth, who are deeply rooted in the culture and piety
of the people and moulded by the spirit of the age'.[15] It is
not they who gain favour in the eyes of God. Rather, it's
those who have chosen to have nothing, the followers who
have thrown personal security to the winds, who have
neither possessions nor any accepted place in society – these
are the people Jesus called the 'blessed' ones.

These are the people who enjoy illumination, the 'beats'
according to Jesus; they refuse to be in tune with prevailing
fashion or to accommodate themselves to the world's
standards.

> While the world keeps holiday they stand aside, and
> while the world sings 'Gather ye rose-buds while ye may',
> they mourn. They see that for all the jollity on board, the
> ship is beginning to sink. The world dreams of progress,
> of power and of the future, but the disciples meditate on
> the end, the last judgement and the coming of the king-
> dom.[16]

And so Bonhoeffer continues to expound the meaning of
the Beatitudes, showing how the merciful, the pure in heart,
the peacemakers, those who hunger for justice and those
who've been persecuted are all blessed in the eyes of God.
*The Cost of Discipleship* begins with a famous sentence:
'Cheap grace is the deadly enemy of our Church. We are
fighting for costly grace.' Those whom he calls the blessed
have understood this distinction and received illumination.

'Cheap grace', Bonhoeffer announced on the very first
page, 'means grace sold on the market like cheapjack's

wares. The sacraments, the forgiveness of sin, and the consolations of religion thrown away at cut prices . . . Cheap grace means grace as a doctrine, a principle, a system.'[17] Kerouac and his friends would have offered ready sympathy for such an observation.

Costly grace, meanwhile, is the pearl of great price for which a merchant will sell all his goods. 'It is *costly* because it calls us to follow, and it is *grace* because it calls us to follow *Jesus Christ*. It is costly because it costs a man his life, and it is grace because it gives a man the only true life.'[18]

The German edition of this book had appeared in 1937. At that time, Bonhoeffer had already shown himself ready to stand in opposition not only to the increasingly strident National Socialism of the Third Reich but also to the toadying collusion of the National Church. In 1933, when Hitler came to power, he abandoned his academic career, which seemed to him to have lost its meaning. He went on to direct an illegal church training college in Finkenwalde near Stettin, a college whose students lived in community in a spirit of brotherhood. By 1935 he was one of the leaders of the confessing Church; in a radio broadcast, he denounced a political system that corrupted and grossly misled the nation and was intent on making the Führer its idol and God.

Bonhoeffer's book was written at the height of this pre-war phase of the struggle with Nazism. It expressed his vision well enough but, for all its clarity of purpose and even its prophetic note, it remained the utterance of a well-connected and privileged young man who might always be supposed capable of 'pulling rank' if he were ever to get into trouble. The irresistible challenge, the overwhelmingly powerful impact, of *The Cost of Discipleship* sprang in the end from events rather than merely the quality of its contents. The key moment in this development, the turning point in Bonhoeffer's life, occurred in June 1939.

He was in New York and facing a very difficult decision. Influential friends wanted him to stay in the United States to lecture and write and also to work with German refugees. The situation in Germany, meanwhile, was getting worse by the day and Bonhoeffer was on edge. 'I have made a mistake in coming to America,' he wrote in his diary; 'I must live through this difficult period of our national history with the Christian people of Germany. I will have no right to participate in the reconstruction of Christian life in Germany after the war if I do not share the trials of this time with my people . . . Christians in Germany will face the terrible alternative of either willing the defeat of their nation in order that Christian civilization may survive, or willing the victory of their nation and thereby destroying our civilisation. I know which of these alternatives I must choose; but I cannot make that choice in security.'[19]

And so, to the disappointment of his friends and backers, he went home. From the same city that offered Sal Paradise and Dean Moriarty a point of departure for their 'overburst of American joy' when taking to the road in search of the wide open spaces and all the adventures of life, from that very same New York, the young Dietrich Bonhoeffer went in the opposite direction. In his case, too, the search was for freedom. For him, too, the road he was taking would bring experiences he could never have anticipated. It would lead to a prison cell and a miserable itinerary that would end in Flossenburg and death at the end of a rope. Bonhoeffer little knew when he took that fateful decision in June 1939 how he would soon be pushed to his own 'limit experience' and, like Michel Foucault all those years later, find himself hammering out his new understandings of life on the anvil of prison life and in the company of criminals of one sort or another. How would the Beat Generation have responded to these words written to his parents by way of farewell: 'I don't just want to live, but to do the most I can with my life. Since this must now happen through my death, I have made friends with it also . . . It is . . . a much clearer obligation to die than to live in disordered times.' In June 1939, all these events still lay ahead of him. Here was a rich young man who took a fateful decision and thereby gave up all his possessions for the sake of the kingdom.

In the end, it was his death at the hands of the Nazis that gave *The Cost of Discipleship* its awesome authority. His martyrdom put a gloss on the concept of 'costly grace' that had been missing before, and it threw a spotlight on Bonhoeffer's life and work that made him truly a prophet for our times. His *Letters and Papers from Prison* appeared in 1953 and became an instant classic. Included within its pages were poems that burned with all the same passionate intensity as Allen Ginsberg's 'Howl'. Bonhoeffer, too, had seen the best minds of his generation destroyed. Including, of course, his own.

I hear, I hear
The silent thoughts
Of my fellow sufferers asleep or awake,
As if voices, cries,
As if shouts for planks to save them.
I hear the uneasy creak of the beds,
I hear chains.

I hear how sleepless men toss and turn,
Who long for freedom from deeds of wrath.
When at grey dawn sleep finds them
They murmur in dreams of their wives and children.

I hear the sighs and weak breath of the old,
Who in silence prepare for the last journey.
They have seen justice and injustice come and go;
Now they wish to see the imperishable, the eternal.

The good, the bad,
Whatever we have been,
We men of many scars,
We the witnesses of those who died,
We the defiant, we the despondent,
The innocent, and the much accused,
Deeply tormented by long isolation . . .[20]

These lines from 'Night Voices in Tegel' were written in his prison cell in July 1944. They resonate with the same deep pathos as Ginsberg's poem written on a psychiatric ward. And where the Beat poet railed against his Moloch, the depersonalizing forces of capitalism, Bonhoeffer took his stance over against the cruelties of Nazi totalitarianism. He saw clearly how the prevailing political and military and (to a large extent) religious forces had conspired to impose their abomination of desolation upon the world. Bonhoeffer went well beyond railing at this his own Moloch, of course; he joined others in an attempt to overthrow it. The failed attempt on Hitler's life in March 1943 did indeed see some of Germany's best minds destroyed. For all that, however, this last chapter of Bonhoeffer's life left a rich legacy.

Few had seen the collusion between organized Christianity and Nazism at closer quarters than Bonhoeffer. Far from driving him out of faith, however, or into the arms of another religion, it impelled him to do some fundamental thinking about the nature of faith in general and the Christian faith in particular. From his prison cell, he began to work at a new theme. He wanted to find a way to talk about faith in a 'non-religious' way. He became less and less interested in which parts of the creed were still acceptable or meaningful and much more drawn to the question of who Christ is for us today. And, at this point, there is a close similarity between the spirituality of the Beats and the spirit of Bonhoeffer. As he put it:

> If our final judgement must be that the Western form of Christianity, too, was only a preliminary stage to a complete absence of religion, what kind of situation emerges for us, for the Church? How can Christ become the Lord of the religionless world as well? . . . How do we speak of God – without religion, i.e. without the temporally conditioned presuppositions of metaphysics, inwardness, and so on? How do we speak (or perhaps we cannot now even 'speak' as we used to) in a 'secular' way about 'God'? In what way are we 'religionless-secular' Christians, in what way are we the *ekklesia*, those who are called forth, not regarding ourselves from a religious point of view as specially favoured, but rather as belonging wholly to the world? In that case Christ is no longer an object of religion, but something quite different, really the Lord of the world. But what does that mean?[21]

He went on to answer the question he'd posed. The lordship of Christ, he argued, is saved from clericalization and hierarchical tendencies because this Lord exercises his lordship always and solely through powerlessness, service and the cross. From his prison cell, deprived of all contact with the Church and all formal religion, he sets himself the task of learning how the suffering and powerless Christ becomes the defining, liberating and creative centre of the world we live in.

For a start, he delighted in the new secularization of 'a world come of age.' He disliked the condemnatory, negative way the Church had tended to speak of it. For him, it was necessary to work out a 'theology of the cross' that addressed the secular world with total seriousness. It would be interesting to know just what the Beats, seeking truth within the teachings of Buddha, would have made of the paradoxes to which Bonhoeffer was driven in his attempt to get to the heart of this question:

> Our coming of age leads us to a true recognition of our situation before God. God would have us know that we must live as people who manage our lives without him. The God who is with us is the God who forsakes us (Mark 15:34). The God who lets us live in the world without the working hypothesis of God is the God before whom we stand continually. Before God and with God we live without God. God lets himself be pushed out of the world on to the cross. He is weak and powerless in the world, and that is precisely the way, the only way, in which he is with us and helps us.[22]

And he concludes that it is the process of secularization itself that has contributed towards the world's coming of age and delivered us from all false conceptions of God (especially 'religious' ones!) and opened up a way of seeing the God of the Bible who wins power and space in the world by his weakness.

In all this searching for meaning in times of chaotic disorder, he sometimes found himself at a loss to hang on to himself. He tried hard to keep up an outward appearance of calm but, in his quieter moments, wondered how to deal with his inner turmoil. This left him asking the most fundamental question of them all:

Who am I? They often tell me
I stepped from my cell's confinement
calmly, cheerfully, firmly,
like a Squire from his country house.

Who am I? They often tell me
I used to speak to my warders
freely and friendly and clearly,
as though it were mine to command.

Who am I? They also tell me
I bore the days of misfortune
equably, smilingly, proudly,
like one accustomed to win.

Am I then really that which other men tell of?
Or am I only what I myself know of myself?
Restless and longing and sick, like a bird in a cage,
struggling for breath, as though hands were compressing
   my throat,
yearning for colours, for flowers, for the voices of birds,
thirsting for words of kindness, for neighbourliness,
tossing in expectation of great events,
powerlessly trembling for friends at an infinite distance,
weary and empty at praying, at thinking, at making,
faint, and ready to say farewell to it all.

Who am I? This or the Other?
Am I one person today and tomorrow another?
Am I both at once? A hypocrite before others,
and before myself a contemptible woebegone weakling?
Or is something within me still like a beaten army
fleeing in disorder from victory already achieved?

Who am I? They mock me, these lonely questions of
   mine.
Whoever I am, Thou knowest, O God, I am thine!

While the last line of this poem might seem too triumph-alist by far in view of the previous tortured self-questioning, it was finally vindicated by the way Bonhoeffer faced his death. On Sunday, 8 April 1945, just weeks before the end of the war, he held a little service for a number of his fellow prisoners. As a captured British officer who was present recalled: 'He had hardly finished his last prayer when the door opened and two evil-looking men in civilian clothes came in and said: "Prisoner Bonhoeffer, get ready to come with us." Those words "come with us" – for all prisoners they had come to mean one thing only – the scaffold. We bade him goodbye – he drew me aside – "This is the end," he said, "for me the beginning of life." Next day at Flossenburg he was hanged.'

Or, in the words of the camp doctor who recalled the event ten years later: 'At the place of execution, he said a short prayer and then climbed the steps to the gallows, brave and composed. His death ensued after a few seconds. In the almost 50 years that I worked as a doctor, I have hardly ever seen a man die so entirely submissive to the will of God.'

---

## Questions for discussion

1. Is it really possible to see blessedness in the down-and-out? Or is that a romantic illusion? Is it true that the Church tends to respond to the poor and downbeat either by ignoring them or by offering them condescension or paternalism? If there is any truth in this, what do we need to do to get our attitudes and our actions right?

2. Is Christianity so tarnished by its association with a civilization that many people think of as materialistic and imperialistic that we're in danger of driving people into the arms of other groups and lifestyles that may be perceived to be 'purer' or 'better'? And if this is indeed the case, how on earth do we re-establish our freedom and integrity?

3. Is faith possible without religion? Is Bonhoeffer's martyrdom so pure and awesome that it becomes unhelpful for us as we try to live our ordinary everyday lives? Or, by going the full distance, did he in fact show us aspects of the life of faith that we dare not lose or run away from?

# 2

# Through bars of rage: the not-always-Swinging Sixties

The 1960s are widely acknowledged to have set in train some kind of social revolution. I must say that much of it passed me by. I recall how William Wordsworth described the way he wrote his poetry. It wasn't, he said, a case of writing down his impressions spontaneously but far more a matter of waiting and allowing experiences he'd been impressed by to permeate his whole being. Stretched out on his bed, 'in vacant or in pensive mood', he would ruminate about things he'd seen and heard. Then, and only then, his poetry would emerge, a matter of 'emotion recollected in tranquillity'. And that's pretty much how I've come to work out what was happening through those years of momentous change. It all swirled around me; some of it drew me in and a great deal failed to stir either an interest or stimulate a response. At the time. But I've brooded over it all a great deal since.

Two books sum up a great deal of the 1960s. One, a little red book containing the *Thoughts of Chairman Mao*, a little crackerjack that urged people to spark and sparkle with revolutionary fire, was wielded by the Red Brigades who implemented China's Cultural Revolution in the middle of the decade. 'A revolution', it declared, 'is not a dinner party, or a writing an essay, or painting a picture, or doing embroidery . . . a revolution is an insurrection, an act of violence by which one class overthrows another.' In another place, it asserted that 'truth comes out of the barrel of a gun'. This small book incited students and workers alike to radical action and contributed significantly to the campus riots and social and political upheavals across the western world. Allied to such thinking was the romantic heroism of Che Guevara who, in the period following the Cuban revolution that brought Fidel Castro to power in 1959, went to Latin America to spread the struggle further afield. His death there in 1967 and the almost Christ-like image of him that was blazoned across tee-shirts and news-papers made him a cult figure, an icon of his age. Fanned by such organizations as the Campaign for Nuclear Dis-armament and the Socialist Workers Movement, campus life seemed at the mercy of heady forces from the left. Once again, William Wordsworth might have spoken for many who found all this invigorating stuff when he wrote, in response to the French Revolution of 1789: 'Bliss was it in that dawn to be alive and to be young was very heaven.' All that fervour is well-recounted in Sheila Rowbotham's *Promise of a Dream*, which tells how a great deal of the energy put into 'ban the bomb' demonstrations during those years was the product of a conviction that the world could end within a few years. Rowbotham goes on to suggest that the 'chiliastic spirit' behind these attitudes was later to find its way into the counter-culture and eventually into environmental politics.[1]

The other book that left its mark on this generation was D. H. Lawrence's *Lady Chatterley's Lover*. Written at the beginning of the century, this novel had appeared in an unexpurgated version only in France where it was brought out as long ago as 1929. In 1960, Penguin Press decided to mark the fortieth anniversary of the author's death (and their own twenty-fifth anniversary) by publishing eight Lawrence titles including an unexpurgated version of *Lady Chatterley's Lover*. They certainly took courage from the Obscene Publications Act, which had come onto the statute book in July 1959 and allowed 'literary merit' as a possible defence against prosecution for obscenity. The success of Allen Ginsberg's 'Howl' in the American courts a few years earlier must also have encouraged them.

When, in due course, the Director of Public Prosecutions decided to bring an action against the Lawrence book the stage was set for one of the defining moments in the evolution of a post-war culture. The trial took place at the Old Bailey over the space of five days in November 1960. The four-letter words, explicit sexual references, frequent descriptions of male and female genitalia and the frank details of a scene involving buggery gave the prosecution the material they thought they needed to pursue a successful case. But a range of witnesses from John A. T. Robinson, the Bishop of Woolwich, to Richard Hoggart, the renowned literary critic, was called by the defence and they made a strong case for the book on the grounds of its literary merit. The whole thing almost turned into farce with the assinine observations of the prosecution barrister Mervyn Griffith-Jones. 'Would you approve of your young sons, young daughters – because girls can read as well as boys – reading this book?' he asked. 'Is it a book that you would have lying around in your own house? Is it a book that you would even wish your wife or your servants to read?'

Permission to publish was granted and two million copies of the book were sold within a year of the trial. The stage was set for an exponential growth in printed and other materials to address the seemingly insatiable needs of a generation desperate to feed its long-repressed sexual fantasies and gratify its carnal longings. This, together with the contraceptive pill, the implementation of the Wolfenden report's recommendations for a more liberal approach to homosexual activity and the legalization of abortion, represented a sexual revolution heavily criticized by some, loudly applauded by others. The permissive society had come. For women, people with a same-sex orientation, and anyone wanting to explore and enjoy sexual activity without the traditional linkage of such experience to marriage, this was a new age of freedom. For the most part, the Church didn't (and still doesn't) have a clue how to deal with it.

The debate surrounding the appearance of these books represented attitudes very evident throughout society. No one enjoyed or exploited the new freedoms of these times more than 'pop artist' Andy Warhol. By the 1960s, Warhol had moved from the world of advertising (where he'd made a great deal of money) to the founding of an art movement which ousted the various forms of Abstract Expressionism and 'painterly art' that had previously dominated the scene. Instead, with his distinctive form of pop art based on silk-screen reproduction and the bludgeoning use of repetition, he made himself famous. He enjoyed the limelight, was lionized by the 'beautiful people' of the time, developed a cult of the personality, and remained enigmatic to the end. While giving the impression of creating a counter-culture it was clear, in fact, that his 'underground' activities were little more than bohemian or fringe, avant-garde or experimental. They were never really a threat, nor intended to be, to the status quo. Indeed, Warhol's greatest gift was that of a very traditional entrepreneur. Self-publicity and a capacity to shock got him everywhere. The rich and famous loved him and he appeared at all the leading social events.

Warhol's 'Factory' in New York attracted all kinds of people – artists, college students, celebrities, New York lowlife, drug users, homosexuals and photographers who documented the scene. Here, he mass-produced his depictions of such unlikely objects as dollar bills, Campbell's soup tins, Coca-Cola bottles, hamburgers and comic book characters, all in endless repetition. What's more, he produced portraits of some of the most iconic figures of the age: Marilyn Monroe, Mick Jagger, Princess Caroline, Truman Capote and Michael Jackson. All these and others were given the silk-screen treatment.

Warhol constantly created a furore for his readiness to flaunt his homosexuality and his inclination, through film as well as art, to give jejune and boring aspects of life (like sleeping, for example), their 'fifteen minutes of fame'. The FBI were constantly examining his work and this, of course, simply contributed to his fame and gave the rich and famous a frisson of excitement at being known to keep his company. In 1968, the year when Martin Luther King and Robert Kennedy were assassinated, Warhol himself came within an ace of a similar fate. Indeed, it was the day before Kennedy was killed that Valeria Solanas, a psychologically disturbed woman and occasional visitor to the Factory, best known for her SCUM manifesto (SCUM being the 'Society for Cutting Up Men'), shot him at close range and almost killed him. After his recovery he continued to outrage and delight people in equal measure but it's arguable that this experience of near-death was a defining moment for him. It made him more withdrawn and even morbid. This fear of death stayed with him until the end. He died in hospital after a routine operation in 1987. It was very clear at the Tate Modern's Warhol Exhibition in the early part of 2002, that he continues to be considered a very important shaper of the culture of the late twentieth century. More people attended this exhibition than went to the Queen Mother's funeral.

Andy Warhol is an easy figure to caricature; this wig-wearing, apparently cold observer, detached and even callous while others were self-destructing around him, can easily be turned into a man of straw to knock down at will. But, as usual, the truth is much more complex. His silent, observing role may well have had as much to do with his dreadful shyness as anything else. While he undoubtedly kept a studied and enigmatic detachment from the crowds who flocked around him, there was another aspect of his life that showed a quite different aspect to his character. He regularly turned up to help at the shelter for the homeless run by the Church of the Heavenly Rest in New York. The rector of the church wrote of the dedicated regularity with which he'd come to the Fifth Avenue church hall to pour coffee, serve food and help clean up for the large number of homeless people, many of them dishevelled and disturbed. 'More than that,' continued the rector, 'he was a true friend to these friendless. He loved these nameless New Yorkers and they loved him back.'

Clearly, Andy Warhol shared the attraction of the Beat Generation to the poor and downtrodden. Indeed, a number of these seem to have been among those who frequented the Factory. He didn't seem to want to keep the psychiatrically disturbed or the deviants and misfits of society away. It was one such person who shot him and this led to a serious re-evaluation of his open house policy. In a rare interview, later in his life, he described his reflections thus:

> It [the shooting] put a new perspective on my memories of all the nutty people I had spent so much time with; crazy people had always fascinated me because they were so creative – they were incapable of doing things normal-

ly . . . usually they would never hurt anybody, they were just disturbed themselves; but how would I ever know again which was which? The fear of getting shot again made me think that I'd never again talk to somebody whose eyes looked weird. But when I thought about that, I got confused, because it included almost everybody I really enjoyed.[2]

These words, describing Warhol's own understanding of the 'limit experience', might well have been written by Michel Foucault.

And so we note the altruistic side of Andy Warhol's character with some interest. Even more fascinating is the way he clung to a devotional life and to the religion of his youth. He said his prayers, attended mass, paid for the studies of a nephew entering the priesthood right to the end of his life. Jane Daggett Dillenberger's fine book about Warhol's religious art is an eye-opener on this subject. He was born in 1928 in a two-room dwelling in Pittsburgh to parents who had been immigrants from the Slovak Republic in the former Czechoslovakia. They joined other members of the Ruthenian community in Pittsburgh who looked to the Byzantine Catholic Church to maintain a sense of identity in their new land. They were very faithful church attenders and Warhol was brought up strictly within the old traditions. While he sat in church he would have gazed at the amazingly colourful iconostasis with its pictures of the saints and martyrs of the church, a whole host of visual images to feed and stimulate a young mind. There were also icons at home.

Warhol's father died in 1942 and the whole family endured great hardship for a number of years. Once he'd moved to New York and begun to make money, he brought his mother to live with him and they remained together virtually until her death in 1972. Throughout this time, he maintained a religious life even though he would have heard sermons preached at the church he attended that repeatedly and insistently condemned homosexuality. This led him, in the end, to lurk on the edge of the congregation – he'd attend mass with the same regularity as he'd always done but without taking communion.

The eulogy delivered at the memorial service for Warhol held at St Patrick's Cathedral in New York City focused on his affection for the religion of his youth and his devotional life. 'The knowledge of this secret piety,' the speaker said, 'inevitably changes our perception of an artist who fooled the world into believing that his only obsessions were money, fame, glamour, and that he was cool to the point of callousness. Never take Andy at face value. The callous observer was in fact a recording angel.'³

The programme for this service was illustrated with a reproduction of one of Warhol's well-known religious paintings *Raphael 1–6.99*. It is based on Raphael's well-known *Sistine Madonna*, a highly devotional portrayal of the Virgin Mary and her child. The picture is dominated by a large and colourful price tag showing the figures $6.99. This incongruous item with its bright yellow figures against a scarlet background seems to turn a traditional religious image into a cheap commodity that can be bought across a counter. He achieves a similar effect in another of his pictures, this time based on Leonardo da Vinci's well-known and much-hackneyed *Last Supper*. The artist superimposes a garish and unlikely picture of a motorcycle across the familiar table scene, a detail that shocks by its sheer unexpectedness. As Dillenberger observes,

> Warhol's juxtaposition here of the Christ of Leonardo with the motorcycle, our age's symbol of untrammelled

freedom, power, and sexuality, results in a brash and commanding painting. Two sides of Warhol, his piety and his deep involvement in aspects of our culture that are inimical to that piety, are here asserted and held in an unresolved tension.[4]

And that same unresolved tension lies at the heart of many people in the modern world. We embrace the freedoms of a permissive age, enjoying the opportunities for pleasure and new experience it affords, without really kicking the habit of our old pieties. A burgeoning and bewildering range of 'spiritualities' beckons us, offering to satisfy our deep yearnings and unanswered questions. 'Religion', on the other hand, leaves large numbers cold. The institutional Church drives them, as it drove Warhol, to (or more usually beyond) its margins. Its cold and formal stance, its moralizing disapproval, seem light years from their everyday lives and needs. Bookshops offer a good indicator of this tension. Where we used to see a section marked 'Religion', we now find 'Body, Mind and Spirit'. In a shop I visited recently, I noted six bays, five feet or so wide and ten shelves tall. On offer was an extraordinary menu of spiritual delights. The options were clearly marked as follows:

**Bay One:**   Astrology, Chinese astrology, Psychics, Channelling, Life after Death

**Bay Two:**   Nostradamus, Divination and Prophecy, Pendulums, Runes, Feng Shui, I Ching, Tarot, Dreams

**Bay Three:** Myths and Legends, Sacred Places, British Mythology, Celtic Myth, Arthurian, Witchcraft

**Bay Four:**  Holistic, Self-help, Shamanism

| Bay Five: | Spiritual Masters, Castaneda, Louise Hay, Krishnamurti, Meditation, T'ai Chi, Auras, Hypnosis, Chakras, Colour Healing, Crystals |
|-----------|------------------------------------------------------------------------------------------------------------------------------------|
| Bay Six:  | Comparative Religion: Buddhism, Hinduism, Judaism, Islam, Sufism, Zen |

This seems to me to offer conclusive proof that people continue to be preoccupied with spiritual matters. The absence of Christianity from the list was striking.

Another significant person who seemed during these years to embody this unresolved tension between the hedonistic and often ephemeral aspects of contemporary culture on the one hand and the ongoing and unquenchable need for some kind of spirituality on the other was George Harrison.

The early 1960s' musical scene was dominated by the Beatles. They commanded huge audiences on both sides of the Atlantic and generated a following never previously seen. They came across as an ordinary bunch of lads and their music seemed so very natural. In a sense, as one critic put it, they gave music back to the people. A succession of hits appeared year after year and their popularity reached well beyond the teenagers who screamed their adoration at airports, outside hotels, and wherever they could get a sight of their heroes.

It is worth noting that the group chose to spell its name in the way they did out of affection for the Beats whom they admired greatly. Soon, every aspect of the lifestyles of these young men was being blazoned abroad in the tabloid newspapers and on television for a public whose appetite for such details seemed insatiable. For all their clean-cut image, the group had availed themselves of the usual sexual opportunities that seemed an inevitable part of the lifestyle of pop

stars and celebrities, especially when they were on tour. But
it was their readiness to use LSD (Lysergic Acid Diethyl-
amide), an hallucinogenic substance that had taken over
from benzedrine as the recreational drug of choice, which
produced some interesting outcomes. Indeed, for George
Harrison the use of LSD proved to be a turning point in his
life. 'Up until LSD,' he declared, 'I never realized that there
was anything beyond this state of consciousness . . . [but]
the first time I took it, it just blew everything away. I had
such an overwhelming feeling of well-being, that there was
a God and I could see Him in every blade of grass . . . LSD
was the key that opened the door to reveal [these profundi-
ties]. From the moment I had that, I wanted to have it all the
time.'5

Thus began George Harrison's search for spiritual truth.
Previously, he may well have subscribed to John Lennon's
off-the-cuff remark that the Beatles had become more
popular than Jesus, or perhaps with Lennon's other observation that, while Jesus was OK, he had no time for all the
nutcases who followed him! But he was now in different
territory. LSD enabled him to take his first step and now, of
all things, it was the sitar (a nine-stringed Indian instrument
with moveable frets and vibrating understrings) that
offered him a second. Other musicians had already experi-
mented with the guitar-like instrument, but when George
Harrison met the hugely respected sitarist Ravi Shankar in
1966, just a few months before the break-up of the Beatles
as a touring group, he knew that he'd found someone who
would mark and shape his whole life. Shankar was master
of his art and Harrison came to understand that 'through
the musical you reach the spiritual'. Shankar insisted that
Harrison should experience India, its culture and pace of
life, if he really wanted to develop his new understandings.
This opened up far more than mere knowledge for 'the

serious Beatle'. It was to lay the foundation of a spirituality that would last to the end of his life.

But it all began, in the words of a recent biographer of Harrison, with 'evidence of half-understood Eastern mysticism and the "psychedelic" inner landscapes of LSD' all mixed up together. Ravi Shankar's tutelage would take Harrison further into the mystery of things. He 'would liken Indian music to "an inner feeling" too intense for satisfactory verbal description: "It's like saying, It's soul, man! . . . [and] when you really get into soul, then . . . it's God."'[6]

Harrison gave himself to the study of Hinduism. He visited sacred sites along the Ganges, learned about Rama and Krishna, studied the Hindu law of karma with its teaching that all evil proceeds from antecedent evil and penalties must be suffered in each succeeding incarnation through which the soul must pass. He came to see this as a necessary process for his own soul. Values in the West were declining, he reckoned, because 'discipline is something we don't like, but in a different way I've found out it's very important, because the only way [Hindu] musicians are great is because they've been disciplined by their guru or teacher and they've surrendered to the person they want to be.'[7]

Harrison was soon to find the fault lines in his new search. Hinduism is a tolerant and gentle faith that advocates pacifism, rejects materialism, shows kindness to animals. All this he found very attractive, but there were aspects of it that were bound to prove difficult for people like him. Wealth and promiscuity and psychedelic drugs as an artificial means to raising awareness (all part of the lifestyle of a pop star) would have been considered obstacles to greater enlightenment, but that didn't stop Harrison composing songs that gave expression to his new-found spirituality. 'Within You Without You', for example, the only solo song on the *Sgt Pepper's Lonely Hearts Club Band* album, lauded love as 'the space between us all' and warned about gaining the world but losing your soul.

Harrison began to speak of his beliefs publicly and this chimed with a number of other artists who were equally ready from the mid-1960s to talk and sing about matters of faith, and the Christian faith at that. Cliff Richard had done a gospel tour as early as 1964. From the Salvation Army had come The Joystrings. A year or two later, songs such as 'Oh Happy Day,' 'Spirit in the Sky,' 'Holy Man' and 'Amazing Grace' sold millions of copies. But Harrison's faith, clearly affected by Hinduism, was assuming a syncretic form in which 'the Lord has a million names'. And all this made him ready to fall into the arms of the Maharishi Mahesh Yogi whom he heard speak in London's Caxton Hall in 1967.

The Maharishi had set up his International Meditation Society as early as 1959 and it already had a membership of 10,000 by the time Harrison came across him. Its attraction lay in the way it offered a meditative method aimed at achieving a pure state of bliss without insisting on the need to give up material possessions or, within reason, worldly pleasures. This seemed the perfect formula for someone like Harrison. It was also the formula with advantages for the Maharishi who suggested that the Beatles tithe a percentage of their income into his Swiss bank account. This was a key factor that led to a parting of the ways between the Liverpool lads and their Indian guru, but only after they'd all, with varying degrees of success, undergone a retreat in India where they undertook lessons in meditation with practical demonstrations, suspended animation and even levitation to consider. Harrison spoke at one point of being in a trance for a 36-hour period. In the end, however, the whole thing ended in failure and it was obvious that Hindu meditative routines were as difficult for Westerners like the Beatles as Buddhist techniques had proved a decade earlier for the Beats.

For a moment, it seemed as if the worlds of pop music and institutional belief might be able to meet and deal with the unresolved tension that had previously made them so suspicious of each other. Edward Patey, Dean of Liverpool Cathedral during the 1970s, praised this apparent coalition of interests as 'the best partnership since the mediaeval duetting of clowns and folk singers.'[8] George Harrison's 'My Sweet Lord' (though later recognized to have been a case of 'subconscious plagiarism') seemed to meet the Dean's bill perfectly. 'My sweet Lord,' it went, 'I really want to see you; I really want to be with you; I really want to see you Lord.' But, for all that, from within the pop world, there was a great deal of criticism at this blending of their kind of music with the concerns of organized belief. As Harrison's biographer puts it,[9] there was an 'overloading of his artistic canvas with the religious preoccupations that were besetting his private life. Once a real cool cat, he was derided by hippies as one more bourgeois liberal with conservative tendencies.' Perhaps, like Andy Warhol, he'd have done better to keep his religious views hidden from view. Instead, he started sermonizing people, giving 'stern dissertations about living a godly life . . . Old at 31, a crashing bore and wearing his virtuous observance of his beliefs like Stanley Green did his sandwich board, he was nicknamed "His Lectureship" behind his back.'[10] None of this deterred this gentle, vegetarian, peace-loving man from the lifestyle he'd chosen, but he couldn't really have claimed to have resolved the tension between life and art, belief and practice, spirituality and pop music.

An unlikely admirer of the Beatles from his California

prison cell was the Black Panther leader Eldridge Cleaver.
He noticed how some white performers had taken the
music of black people and, somehow, succeeded in making
it 'cross over' from one world, one culture, to another. He
recognized Elvis Presley's success in doing this, meeting the
needs of young white people 'whose inner hunger and need
was no longer satisfied with the antiseptic white shoes and
whiter songs of Pat Boone. "You can do anything," sang
Elvis to Pat Boone's white shoes, "but don't you step on my
blue Suede Shoes!"' But Cleaver's admiration for Presley
was not without qualification. He was 'unfunky, mechani-
cal, alienated, too much Body (too soon) . . . [whereas] the
Beatles, affecting the caucasoid crown of femininity and
ignoring the Body on the visual plane (while their music on
the contrary being full of Body)', assuaged all doubts and
met all expectations. They had brought the rhythms and
colours of African American music right into the white
person's world.[11]

Elvis Presley and the Beatles joined Allen Ginsberg and
Jack Kerouac in Eldridge Cleaver's admiration for 'daring
to do in the light of day what America had long been doing
in the sneak-thief anonymity of night – consorted on a
human level with the blacks . . . [As a result of their courage
in doing this, and despite the persecution and contempt
directed at them, they'd held fast to their determination
to make 'the black man's code fit their facts'.] Bing
Crosbyism, Perry Comism, and Dinah Shoreism had led to
cancer, and the vanguard of the white youth knew it.'[12]

These observations are recorded in a very powerful book
by Cleaver, written while he was in prison convicted of
rape, called *Soul on Ice*. I remember reading it shortly after
its publication in 1968 but found it almost unbearable in its
searing honesty and burning anger. Indeed, I found some of
it repulsive and had no critical or emotional tools then to

help me with it – it was brutal, lucid, passionate and pitiless in its unremitting analysis. My difficulties began right at the beginning of the book where Cleaver makes an attempt to explain and justify the acts of rape he'd committed that had led to his imprisonment.

I couldn't then (and can't now) think of any rationale that could possibly excuse rape. To my mind, it falls in the same category of offence as paedophilia and child abuse. I identify with the injunction of Jesus that, for such people, it would be better for them and everyone else if a millstone were tied around their neck and they were thrown into the sea. And that's where the whole matter lay until, just a few months ago when, out of the blue, a friend sent me his copy of *Soul on Ice*. I'd long since disposed of mine. I found myself once again both drawn into Cleaver's argument and frightened by some of his conclusions. This time round, however, I found that I could follow his line of reasoning through to its conclusion. Perhaps I was just older and had seen more of the world.

Cleaver describes the critical path that led to his committing the violent crimes against women for which he'd been convicted. He'd done these things, he said, to expunge the image of the white woman as the ultimate in beauty, untouchable by blacks, and therefore the supreme symbol of white America's hold over its African-American population. He described his feelings when looking at a pin-up of a white woman. 'I looked at the picture again and again,' he wrote, 'and in spite of everything and against my will and the hate I felt for the woman and all that she represented, she appealed to me. I flew into a rage at myself, at America, at white women, at the history that had placed those tensions of lust and desire in my chest.'[13]

The discovery of these feelings, he went on to declare, was like taking a medicine that made him aware of just how much American capitalism deserved all the hatred and contempt that he felt for it in his heart. Indeed, this picture of an America he detested became his own equivalent of Allen Ginsberg's Moloch. It was out of the maelstrom of these feelings of lust and hatred, he alleges, that he was driven to his acts of rape. He felt revulsion for what he was doing but nevertheless went on doing it repeatedly.

Now, in prison, he has plenty of opportunity to reflect on what he's done. Rape, he now recognizes, is an insurrectionary act. 'My pride as a man dissolved,' he wrote, 'and my whole fragile moral structure seemed to collapse, completely shattered'[14] by the enormity of the act. But he was determined to square up to himself and think all these things through. He knew he'd done wrong and was detestable in the eyes of those who'd been affected by his actions, but, beyond that, he knew too that he'd lost his self-respect. Rather than move into denial, he determined to write down the way he'd felt driven to his acts of rape with total honesty. Only by writing, he felt, could he possibly save himself and find out who he was and what he wanted to be.

He knew that the 'white woman/black man' sickness had to be brought out into the open, dealt with and resolved. 'Many whites flatter themselves,' he writes, 'with the idea that the Negro male's lust and desire for the white dream girl is purely an aesthetic attraction, but nothing could be further from the truth. His motivation is often of such a bloody, hateful, bitter, and malignant nature that whites would really be hard pressed to find it flattering.' Now, in prison, he points to the experience of men convicted of rape, experience that, rather than simply to be abhorred, should somehow be utilized to help other youngsters who might be heading in the same direction. 'I think all of us, the entire nation,' he writes, 'will be better off if we bring it all out front. A lot of people's feelings will be hurt, but that is the price that must be paid.' And the conclusion he comes to as he brings his painful and uncomfortable chapter to an end is stark and simple: 'The price of hating other human beings is loving oneself less.'[15]

Cleaver recognizes that much of his thinking is triggered by a visceral hatred of white people. During his first spell in prison, he'd become a Christian. He was baptized and then confirmed as a Roman Catholic. He attended mass and went to confession, said his rosary and wore a cross round his neck. He'd decided to be a Catholic because that's where the Mexicans and other Hispanics in jail were to be found. The Protestant cause attracted only whites. But soon Christianity palled on him. He converted to the Nation of Islam, more popularly known as the Black Muslims. This movement, headed by the Honourable Elijah Muhammad and his spokesman El-Hajj Malik El-Shabazz (Malcolm X), was attracting large numbers of disenchanted black people especially from society's misfits and no-hopers. Mohammed Ali (previously known as Cassius Clay) had been a high-profile convert who, by his achievements and by his readiness to reject the draft, had inspired many African Americans to believe in themselves. 'I ain't got no quarrel with them Viet Congs,' he had said and this was echoed by Cleaver who complained that black men were the biggest fools on earth if they were prepared to go to another country (Vietnam) to fight for what they themselves didn't have. The rejection of Christian America by the Nation of Islam was an indictment of what they understood to be a racist and inherently oppressive system.

Thomas Merton, a Trappist monk, had written a paragraph about life in Harlem, a piece that had so captivated Cleaver that he copied it out and used it again and again when giving Black Muslim lectures to his fellow inmates. It makes its own point:

> Here in this huge, dark, steaming slum, hundreds of thousands of Negroes are herded together like cattle, most of them with nothing to eat and nothing to do. All the senses and imagination and sensibilities and emotions and sorrows and desires and hopes and ideas of a race with vivid feelings and deep emotional reactions are forced in upon themselves, bound inward by an iron ring of frustration: the prejudice that hems them in with its four insurmountable walls. In this huge cauldron, inestimable natural gifts, wisdom, love, music, science, poetry are stamped down and left to boil with the dregs of an elementally corrupted nature, and thousands upon thousands of souls are destroyed by vice and misery and degradation, obliterated, wiped out, washed from the register of the living, dehumanized.
>
> What has not been devoured, in your dark furnace, Harlem, by marijuana, by gin, by insanity, hysteria, syphilis?[16]

The anger, raw and undifferentiated, needs to be heard and felt by everyone for what it is. Much lip-service is paid to the cause of anti-racism by people who haven't really appreciated the compounded sense of alienation that consumes so many black people. But Cleaver went beyond mere anger. By looking open-eyed into his own soul he began to wrestle with the need to beat out plough shares of hope on the anvil of his own despair. As we've seen, he thought that a readiness to look at his own horrible deeds might contribute to such a process. He noticed with approval how his hero Malcolm X, after his visit to Mecca and the Middle East, had changed perceptibly. He'd been

'liberated from a doctrine of hate and racial supremacy . . .
[and began] . . . to denounce the racist strait-jacket demon-
ology of Elijah Muhammed'.[17] Cleaver took Malcolm X's
side in the increasingly bitter dispute that soon divided the
Black Muslims.

The alienation of young people evoked deep sympathy
from Cleaver. He recognized in their radical anger a reson-
ance with some of the feelings held by his fellow African-
Americans. Indeed, he described the plight of young people
and the rift between the generations as 'deeper, even, than
that between the races'. Young whites had lost their heroes.
The heroes of their history were being shown up to have
gained their plaudits by 'erecting the inglorious edifice of
colonialism and imperialism.' Indeed, young people were
'experiencing the great psychic pain of waking into consciousness to find their inherited heroes turned by events
into villains.'[18] This had driven a wedge between young
people and their parents and had radicalized the anger and
alienation on both sides. People like Jack Kerouac had
understood this but he too was derided by the older and
more traditional America.

His ringing conclusion to this analysis is uncompromis-
ing. 'A young white today', he writes, 'cannot help but
recoil from the base deeds of his people. On every side, on
every continent, he sees racial arrogance, savage brutality
toward the conquered and subjugated people, genocide; he
sees the human cargo of the slave trade; he sees the system-
atic extermination of American Indians; he sees the civilized nations of Europe fighting in imperial depravity over
the lands of other people – and over possession of the very
people themselves. There seems to be no end to the ghastly
deeds of which his people are guilty. GUILTY. The slaugh-
ter of the Jews by the Germans, the dropping of atomic
bombs on the Japanese people – these deeds weigh heavily

upon the prostrate souls and tumultuous consciences of the white youth. The white heroes, their hands dripping with blood, are dead.'[19]

Like his hero, Malcolm X, Cleaver became interested in finding a more placatory tone. After being caustic about the efforts of Martin Luther King to organize a campaign of non-violent protest against a society that denied blacks their human rights, calling him 'the Booker Washington of his day' (an appeaser), he came later to a different conclusion. When King called on Congress to stop bombing Vietnam and to enter into negotiations with the Viet Cong and also to recognize communist China, thus echoing the demands of the American peace movement, Cleaver acknowledged the establishment of a new alignment of political forces with a radical edge and considerable influence. When President Kennedy addressed the nation after the Birmingham Revolt in the summer of 1963 and sent his bill of rights to congress, something 'unprecedented' had taken place. He gave King credit for this.

These signs of hope within a book that is so uncompromisingly fierce in its analysis of Western values and 'white' civilization are significant. They allow the reader to see how, by allying itself to radical forces of the day, Christian society could redeem itself. This was a line taken up again and again by Martin Luther King himself.

King had had to deal with the 'Black Power' groups who wanted to abandon his own methods of voicing protest in favour of violence. While respecting the sincerity of many of those who wanted to go down that road, he suggested that this was a course 'born from the wounds of despair and disappointment. It was a cry of daily hurt and persistent pain.'[20] He could identify with these feelings and, indeed, had had more than enough experience of them in his own life and ministry.

The nadir point for King must surely have been when he'd gone to Birmingham to organize a demonstration there. He was arrested and thrown into prison and, at one point, placed in solitary confinement. While there, a letter to the local newspaper was brought to his attention. It had been signed by eight of the city's religious leaders including a rabbi. The letter criticized King for interfering in affairs that were none of his business; it declared his visit to Birmingham to be untimely and accused King of contemplating 'unChristian' deeds in his apparent readiness to break the law of the land. The writers pleaded with those organizing the demonstration to call it off and go away. Full rights for black people, they suggested, would come in the fullness of time. It was unnatural (and risked public order) to force the pace with direct action.

King was bitterly disappointed by this letter. It was, after all, written by fellow Church ministers and this undoubtedly got under his skin. It moved him to write his famous letter from jail, a long missive that must be considered among the finest of Martin Luther King's writings. He expressed his deep disappointment that it should have been Church leaders who'd chosen to criticize him in this way. (Billy Graham had on another occasion voiced the same kind of criticism.) He'd have expected their support, he said, rather than their objections. The Church risks losing 'its authenticity, [it will] forfeit the loyalty of millions and be dismissed as an irrelevant social club with no meaning for the twentieth century. Every day I meet young people whose disappointment with the Church has turned into outright disgust. Perhaps I have once again been too optimistic. Is organized religion too inextricably bound to the status quo to save our nation and the world?'[21]

That is precisely the conclusion Jack Kerouac, Andy Warhol, George Harrison and Eldridge Cleaver had come to already. They had either been marginalized, or rejected, by organized Christianity. In a formidable reply to his pusillanimous critics, cowards all of them in his view, King marshalled the views of one theological heavyweight after another. St Augustine, St Thomas Aquinas, Martin Buber, Paul Tillich, Martin Luther and John Bunyan were all wheeled in. His attack on 'white moderates' who ask him to be patient and compliant is withering. How dare those who have never had to endure oppression ask the oppressed to be patient? How long will his critics 'remain silent behind the anaesthetizing security of stained-glass windows?'

He explained how he was trying to hold the middle ground between those blacks who, after years of oppression, had adjusted to segregation and simply accepted their lot and, at the other extreme, those in the black nationalist camp (he mentioned Elijah Muhammad's 'Muslim' movement) whose frustration had led them to lose 'faith in America, to repudiate Christianity, and to conclude that the white man is an incorrigible "devil".' He claimed that he had stuck to his non-violent stance despite being labelled an Uncle Tom by some of his fellow blacks. But he remained convinced 'that if our white brothers dismiss those who employ non-violent direct action as "rabble-rousers" and "outside agitators", and if they refuse to support such action, then millions of Negroes will, out of frustration and despair, seek solace and security in black nationalist ideologies – a development that would inevitably lead to a frightening racial nightmare'.

King answered his critics' allegation that he was an 'extremist' by suggesting that Jesus would have earned the same label. Wasn't he, after all, an extremist for love? How else does one interpret 'Love your enemies, bless those who curse you, do good to those who hate you, and pray for those who are spiteful to you and persecute you'? Amos was an extremist for justice, Paul an extremist for the gospel. So, in the end, he was happy enough to accept the word and see it in a positive sense.

King dismissed the accusation that his preoccupation with the struggle to rid the nation of racial and economic injustice was inappropriate on the grounds that these were social issues with which the gospel had no real concern. He retorted (with the same note of disdain as Desmond Tutu was to affect when faced with the same criticism 30 years later): 'I have watched many churches commit themselves to a completely otherworldly religion which makes a strange, unbiblical distinction between body and soul, between the sacred and the secular.'

And so he made no concessions to his critics. He would not stay at home; rather, he intended to go anywhere where he found injustice. He would fight for the rights of his people non-violently and through direct action. He would go to prison if necessary. He would utter his 'thus saith the Lord' wherever the cause took him and whatever force was lined up against him. 'Like Paul,' he said, 'I must constantly respond to the Macedonian call for aid.' It was a powerful apologia. This was no Booker Washington. This was no Uncle Tom.

Someone who worked with Martin Luther King through these years was Maya Angelou. She is a remarkable woman whose life of suffering and whose indomitable spirit have been an inspiration to countless black (and other) people for many years now. In one of the volumes of her autobiography she describes a meeting with Malcolm X. His total rejection at that time of any possible 'deal' with white people was very clear as, indeed, was his dismissal of Christianity as being a white man's religion. He identified the Christian Church (and even Jesus himself) with the institution of slavery. He had no time for Negro leaders who wanted to reach an accommodation with whites and made it clear that only the Nation of Islam could be counted on not to sell black people into slavery again. He wanted total rejection of white culture and control. Maya Angelou confesses her disappointment. She describes how she left Malcolm X 'in a fog of defeat'. She saw how 'black despair was still real' and how none of the problems of black people would be solved until the anger and alienation of the people who trusted the Nation of Islam for its leadership had been dealt with. She offered a different way of resolving this tension.

First of all, she reminded herself that black people had a long history of what she calls 'mercy'. 'During the thirties Depression,' she writes, 'white hobos left freight trains and looked for black neighbourhoods. They would appear hungry at the homes of the last hired and the first fired and were never turned away . . . For centuries we tended, and nursed, often at our breasts, the children of people who despised us. We had cooked the food of a nation of racists, and despite the many opportunities, there were few stories of black servants poisoning white families. If that didn't show mercy, then I misunderstood the word.'[22]

Then, Angelou goes on to spell out just where such mercy came from. 'As for spirituality,' she writes, 'we were Christians. We demonstrated the teachings of Christ. We turned other cheeks so often our heads seemed to revolve on the end of our necks, like old stop-and-go signs. How many times should we forgive? Jesus said seven times seventy. We forgave as if forgiving was our talent. Our church music showed that we believed there was something greater than we, something beyond our physical selves, and that that something, that God, and His Son, Jesus, were always present and could be called "in the midnight hour" and talked to when the "sun raised itself to walk across the morning sky." We could sing the angels out of heaven and bring them to stand thousands thronged on the head of a pin. We could ask Jesus to be on hand to "walk around" our death beds and gather us into "the bosom of Abraham." We told Him all about our sorrows and relished the time when we would be counted among numbers of those who would go marching in. We would walk the golden streets of heaven, eat of the milk and honey, wear the promised shoes and rest in the arms of Jesus, who would rock us and say, "You have laboured in my vineyard. You are tired. You are home how, child. Well done." Oh there was no doubt that we were spiritual.'

This outburst came as a reaction to Jean Genet's play *The Blacks* which, she felt, gave a white foreigner's idea of a people he didn't understand. He'd suggested that black people might be mean and cruel. He'd argued that when imperialism and colonialism eventually crumbled under its own weight, those who'd previously been the oppressed would take the reins and take over from their former masters. And they'd be no better than the people they'd replaced. It was this that made Maya Angelou so mad. She refused to believe that black people could ever be like whites. Their whole history had shown them to be more caring, more respectful, more merciful and more spiritual. She rejected both the nihilistic anger of the black Muslims and the tortuous reasonings of the white intellectual. She herself felt the anger but refused to give in to it. To her mind it was black people who, even though (perhaps because) they'd been denied freedom, had most to say about it. Freedom was their deepest dream, their fondest hope, their most persistent longing. All of which she expressed brilliantly in a simple poem:

A free bird leaps
on the back of the wind
and floats downstream
till the current ends
and dips his wing
in the orange sun rays
and dares to claim the sky.

But a bird that stalks
down his narrow cage
can seldom see through
his bars of rage
his wings are clipped and
his feet are tied
so he opens his throat to sing.

The caged bird sings
with a fearful trill
of things unknown
but longed for still
and his tune is heard
on the distant hill
for the caged bird
sings of freedom.[23]

Or, as Martin Luther King had put it in 1963 at the conclusion of his great 'I have a dream' speech in Washington: 'When we let freedom ring, when we let it ring from every village and every hamlet, from every state and every city, we will be able to speed up that day when all of God's children, black men and white men, Jews and Gentiles, Protestants and Catholics, will be able to join hands and sing in the words of the Old Negro spiritual, "Free at last! free at last! thank God almighty, we are free at last!"'

This chapter began by suggesting that the 1960s offered unprecedented possibilities for finding freedom. People have sought it through revolution or drugs, by gratifying their need for pleasure or by following a spiritual path. Clearly there is no easy fix for what remains an unresolved tension between personal choice and the common good, sensual gratification and the drive for meaning, anger and alienation over against a renewal of society. Organized religion hasn't, on the whole, done well in helping a confused generation deal with these pressures and paradoxes.

---

## Questions for discussion

1. Andy Warhol was loved by celebrities and deeply mistrusted by the Church, but he maintained contact with the life of faith through it all. How should the Church be towards people known to be living 'dubious' lives?

2. Drugs and music offered George Harrison a way into faith. How on earth do we make sense of that? Are we secretly relieved that he didn't end up a Christian?

3. How can white people understand the anger and the alienation of black people? How do they deal with it? Why do so many black people either maintain their Christian faith in black-led churches or else look elsewhere for solace (e.g. the Nation of Islam)?

4. Have white young people really lost their heroes? If they have, what hope is there for them, or for the rest of us?

# 3

# Through this barren land: tough times in Wales

My first job took me, as an assistant lecturer in the English department, to St David's College, Lampeter. That was when, round the corner of a world now long gone, the little market town could still be reached by train and proudly boasted that it belonged to the county of Cardiganshire. I'd gone to teach medieval literature but little did I guess how much Church history I was going to learn in my three wonderfully happy years spent in that remote corner of Wales.

The college was built in 1822 by C. R. Cockerell, the architect responsible for the Ashmolean Museum in Oxford and the Fitzwilliam in Cambridge. Indeed, it greatly resembled an Oxbridge college. It was incorporated by a succession of Royal Charters the first of which was granted by William IV in 1827 but, even prior to that, King George IV had subscribed to its beginnings. The founder of this, the oldest university outside Oxford and Cambridge, was Bishop Burgess of St David's and he and his successors were Visitors to the college right down to the time I went to work there in the mid-1960s.

When I attended my job interview, I became aware at once of a dimension I could never have guessed at. The occasion was chaired by none other than the Archbishop of

Wales, flanked by a bevy of other Welsh bishops, with a desultory professor or two lurking somewhere in the wings. Within Welsh society, 'Church' and 'Chapel' were fiercely differentiated. The Church in Wales, disestablished in 1920, was considered to belong to the rich, to landowners, the well-connected and (horror of horrors!) the English. Ordinary people attended one or another of the countless chapels scattered across the length and breadth of the principality, stern buildings lowering over whole communities, daring them to misbehave. Places with biblical names such as Moriah, Hermon, Jerusalem or Peniel abounded, edifices of 'sepulchral austerity with flamboyant pulpit oratory which preached hell and eternal damnation.'[1] Many were the fruit of the evangelical revival of the eighteenth century, others had been spawned by the great Welsh Revival of the early part of the twentieth. This non-conformity was further defined and refined by language. There were usually Welsh and English counterparts for all the denominations present in every town or village. The chapels undoubtedly kept Welsh culture and the Welsh language alive.

The University of Wales didn't come into existence until late in the nineteenth century. It claimed no kings among its earliest subscribers; indeed, it made the proud claim to have been founded with the miner's (and the quarryman's) penny. Certainly, it was radically different in character and ethos from its more ancient neighbour. There wasn't much love lost between them either as I discovered when I went to take up my new job. Welsh non-conformity bristled with a barely subdued disdain for the Church in Wales. Those who worshipped God in the Welsh language, meanwhile, tended to look a little askance at those whose devotions were conducted in English.

St David's College Lampeter was finding it increasingly difficult to survive as a separate entity. The period following the Second World War saw huge developments in the world of higher education; universities were expected to furnish the skills and stoke up the white heat of technology needed by the country at large. There was little place within this grand scheme for a little liberal arts college bucolically placed in its fastness in West Wales. Whitehall found it an anomaly to support two universities from the public purse. So Lampeter needed to eat humble pie, suspend its own degree-awarding powers, and enter the federal University of Wales. One of the existing colleges was called on to supervise the transitional period. Aberystwyth, the logical place from which to offer such oversight, showed contempt for the proposal. Arguably, the grounds for this refusal were theological; free church Aberystwyth was a fierce redoubt against anglicizing forces and St David's College, Lampeter spoke loudly of such forces. So it was left to the more distant Cardiff to offer its protection to this new entrant to the national university. This move had all the marks of a 'victory' for non-conformity over some demonized Anglican ascendancy. But was it?

These were also the years that began to reveal fault lines within the Welsh free churches. The *cymanfa ganu* and the local and national *eisteddfodau* continued to give an appearance of strength to chapel culture. But the writing was definitely on the wall. I used to preach in Welsh-language chapels (in English) and be thanked profusely by many of those attending simply because, they explained, they could actually understand what was being said! In those days, the pulpit was graced by wonderful oratory but it all seemed to have become so erudite, so theoretical, so distant. Yet it was in these same years that Saunders Lewis, one of the founders of *Plaid Cymru*, the Welsh Nationalist Party, emerged from retirement to project the

Welsh language onto the centre stage and to demand a new and radical re-evaluation of its place in the life of the nation. In 1963, he founded the *Cymdeithas yr Iaith Gymraeg*, the Welsh Language Society, which politicized the question of language and argued that the survival of Welsh should be given a priority higher even than *Plaid Cymru*'s objective of self-government for Wales. This stance attracted thousands of followers especially among university students. The previously non-political Welsh Youth League (the *Urdd Gobaith Cymru*) was stirred into action with protests, demonstrations, petitions and even a 'Free Wales Army', radicalizing the whole debate about Wales, Welshness and the Welsh language. Perhaps Saunders Lewis and his collaborators had foreseen the collapse of the chapels and, fearing for the survival of the language once this traditional prop had been lost, wanted to further its interests by refocusing the forces of Welsh nationalism and taking its concerns into the streets and the media.

The chapels didn't help themselves through all these developments. They had ossified, petrified. Grace had turned to law. Morality was the name of this new legalism and a whole culture evolved that stood in judgement on people's behaviour, especially if it involved pleasure. Dancing, gambling, smoking, sexual mores and, the biggest ogre of them all, the consumption of alcohol became the big issues. The role of the free churches in all this can all be summed up in an incident from Richard Llewellyn's period piece *How Green Was My Valley*. A chapel deacon is interrogating a young woman who, out of wedlock, has become pregnant. He conducts his examination of her with all the flair and cold-bloodedness of Dostoevsky's Grand Inquisitor.

'Your lusts have found you out,' shouted Mr Parry, and thump went his fist on the handrail, 'and you have paid the price of all women like you. Your body was the trap of the Devil and you allowed temptation to visit you. Now you bring an illegitimate child into the world against the commandment of God. Thou shalt not commit adultery. Prayer is wasted on your sort and you are not fit to enter the House of God. You shall be cast forth into the outer darkness until you have learned your lesson. I am a jealous God, and the sins of the fathers shall be visited upon the children unto the third and fourth generation. Meillyn Lewis, do you admit your sin?'[2]

The poor girl does and is then subjected to further humiliation by her pitiless interrogator. It all evokes a memory of William Blake's poem 'The Garden of Love'.

I went to the Garden of Love,
And saw what I never had seen:
A Chapel was built in the midst,
Where I used to play on the green.

And the gates of this Chapel were shut,
And 'Thou shalt not' writ over the door;
So I turned to the Garden of Love
That so many sweet flowers bore;

And I saw it was fillèd with graves,
And tomb-stones where flowers should be;
And priests in black gowns were walking their rounds,
And binding with briars my joys and desires.

All of this led, of course, to a rotting of the very core of Welsh non-conformity. While such energy as existed was poured into the moralizing campaigns against any relaxation of sabbath observance, or extending the opening hours of licensed premises or any form of sexual deviancy, little attention was being given to the sources of spirituality or to a theology for the times of change so evident on all hands. Chapel culture lived on its capital for a generation and then, when the torrents came, the whole edifice collapsed. The drowning adepts of the noble free church tradition had little to offer to a Wales losing the very social and political infrastructure that had bred it.

The rapid industrial developments of the late eighteenth and nineteenth centuries, so well chronicled in the novels of Alexander Cordell (*Rape of the Fair Country*, *Rebecca's Daughters*, *Song of the Earth* and *This Sweet and Bitter Earth*) and Jack Jones (*River out of Eden*), had built a working-class culture based on the traditional mining and metal industries that were later so dramatically to disappear from the scene. The old Dock Authority building in Cardiff bears a fine bas-relief image on one of its walls. Steam engines are puffing and steam ships ploughing their way across the oceans of the world. This picture of the industrial pre-eminence enjoyed by Wales for a brief moment of time, is aptly summed up in the little phrase *Wrth ddwr a thân* (through water and fire), the formula for all this extraordinary success with the massive fortunes it generated.

The sexual revolution of the 1960s and the decline of the traditional industries that began to gather speed at about the same time, left the free churches of Wales high and dry. Adrian Hastings, in his *Religion in Britain 1900–2000*, describes the demise of *The British Weekly*, the newspaper that had been staple reading in non-conformist families for nigh on a century. Whereas, in its early days, it had espoused great causes like the campaign against the Bulgarian atrocities and the place of Britain in the world, its last issue was only too predictably preoccupied with the subject of drink. Such self-indulgence could only lead to collapse. The chapels clung to the Welsh language, claiming to be its champions but, an ironical fact, needing it now to buttress their own attempts at survival. And meanwhile a whole generation was perishing all around them.

Nature abhors a vacuum. The traditional sources of moral authority were bankrupt. There was disintegration only too evidently corroding the very fabric of Welsh culture. Some very different voices emerged from this wasteland. Out of the grim post-industrial landscape and from this bleak moment, a time between paradigms, came some strident sounds full of anger, alienation and irreverence. But was that all they represented?

I 'discovered' The Manic Street Preachers through my children. There seemed something irreverent in the fact that this group of strange young men should have arrogated to themselves the word 'preachers' at all. It wasn't difficult for me to relegate this pop group to the same parts of my brain to which I dismissed other practitioners of rock 'n' roll, but something within urged me to give this particular group a little more consideration. Perhaps that word 'preachers' intrigued me, or possibly I was attracted by the fact that these lads came from Blackwood in the Sirhowy valley. They seemed to create levels of attention that hadn't been achieved by Welsh stars since Tom Jones of Aberdare and Shirley Bassey of Tiger Bay. So I borrowed their albums from my sons and listened gingerly to the raucous sounds that hit my untutored ear.

The music never grabbed me, but the lyrics did. And so too did the character of Nicky Wire, James Dean Bradfield, Sean Moore and Richey Edwards. Unlike many other pop musicians, these men came from stable homes. They were bright, they studied hard in school and college. They had a love–hate relationship with Wales and, after an early contact with the Church, they abandoned it completely. Indeed, religion left them cold. They hated Sundays. One of Richey Edwards' favourite early tracks was John Lydon's 'Religion' from the debut album of a punk group called Public Image Limited. This was described by one commentator as 'a declamatory, anti-Christianity monologue in which the singer tramples over all manner of doctrines'.

As well as religion, the Preachers also hated Thatcherism and what it did to whole communities in valleys like theirs. They were born just after the Aberfan disaster, which saw over 100 children killed when a coal tip slid down on to their school. They grew up just as the coal mines were being shut down and heavy industries wound up. It still breaks the heart of any visitor with imagination who walks down long streets of terraced houses in valley towns to see the serried ranks of 'For Sale' signs ranged outside so many of them. Dozens sometimes. What social disruption, what community despair, lies behind such a phenomenon? And how did organized Christianity address the momentous changes endured within these communities?

It wasn't to the chapels that Wire, Bradfield, Moore and Edwards looked for wisdom or direction. Nor to Blackwood, which they found depressing, a place that would always kill any ambition held by young people like themselves. So these young men turned to learning. Not just to classroom learning but to a literature that rarely features on school syllabuses. 'Libraries gave us power,' they sang in 'A Design for Life' and their reading included Ginsberg, 'the mighty Kerouac', Burroughs, Camus, Sartre, Joyce, O'Casey, Beckett, Wilde, Kafka and Rimbaud. As one commentator put it: one doesn't have to have a PhD to see themes of alienation and the individual on the fringe of society running through these authors.'[3]

Richey Edwards was the brooding (and brilliant) genius

of the group. He rarely gave interviews but the following is very revealing: 'I was doing A-levels,' he said. 'I was learning really fast . . . everything, everywhere. And reading like crazy and we had this intellectual thing going that was beyond the classroom. You know . . . the stuff that was really valuable was stuff that wasn't in the curriculum . . . That's not real education. That's not where wisdom lies. Wisdom lies in seeing beyond that. I got wisdom from Larkin, from Kerouac . . . Jack Kerouac! Fantastic! The most intelligent bloke who ever lived and he saw genius in people who were basically bohos (bohemians). Neal Cassady was the kind of guy who somebody who works at Tesco's might regard as a loser. He was a drunken bum who never held a job and shirked all his responsibilities and yet Kerouac saw the real value in that. To Kerouac, one of the sharpest brains America has produced . . . Cassady was a true hero. That, to me, is just beyond everything that Thatcher's . . . eighties threw up. It was so much wiser, on such a higher plane, than those wankers in the British government.'[4]

The angry sounds made by this valley group soon drew them to the attention of a large audience. They were being mentioned in the same breath as influential groups such as The Clash, The Stone Roses, The Sex Pistols, Nirvana and New Order. It's arguable that their art peaked in 1994 with their album *The Holy Bible*. Once again, the Manics invaded the vocabulary and the iconography of the Church. On the cover of their album the singers were pictured wearing haloes. Images of a grotesquely obese woman by Jenny Saville appeared in triptych form. A collage of other pictures showed a scene of graveyard sculptures full of crosses, angels and popular piety. These provocative images shared space with an equally provocative quotation from Octave Mirabeau's *The Torture Garden*:

You're obliged to pretend respect for people and institutions you think absurd. You live attached in a cowardly fashion to moral and social conventions you despise, condemn, and know lack all foundation. It is that permanent contradiction between your ideas and desires and all the dead formalities and vain pretences of your civilization which makes you sad, troubled and unbalanced. In that intolerable conflict you lose all joy of life and all feeling of personality, because at every moment they suppress and restrain and check the free play of your powers. That's the poisoned and mortal wound of the civilized world.

The very first track sets the tone for the rest. Cascading words falling over each other, everything is passionate and bleak. The song is called 'Yes'. 'I don't know what I'm scared of or what I even enjoy', it declares. Then it goes on to describe the kind of society we live in where money calls the shots. For the right price, you can procure all the pleasures you want, but, when all is said and done, the freedom and power conferred on someone by money remains futile if we can't even say thank you, if we can't shout or scream, if we have to hurt ourselves to 'let the pain out'. This mention of hurting oneself may well have been a reference to a much-publicized act of self-mutilation on the part of Richey Edwards in 1992. He took a razor and, to the horror of the journalist interviewing him, cut the phrase '4 real' across his forearm until it became a bloody mess. This seemed in tune with the song called 'Purgatory's Circle', within whose swirling waters people drown even as others continue to preoccupy themselves with the pleasures money can buy, seemingly oblivious to what's in store for them. It's only once people have fallen into this cycle that anyone thinks of trying to help them. The song ends sardonically:

'Funny place for the social [services] to start caring, just an ambulance at the bottom of a cliff.'

People used to singing hymns to regular metres must grin and bear the irregularity in the patterning of these words. And they must look deeper than the instinctive rejection, the 'things can't be as bleak as that' or the 'pull your socks up' responses. Most of the lyrics on this album were written by Richey Edwards. He was the most fragile and vulnerable member of the group, sensitive and alone. The others, when their fame was on the wane, went back to sedentary living. Edwards took to heavy drinking to anaesthetize the pain of living and facing people; he took to smoking up to 70 cigarettes a day; he suffered from an eating disorder; he mutilated himself, hurt himself deliberately. In early 1995 his car was found abandoned near the Severn Bridge. He has never been seen since. And it would be easy to write him off as a depressive misfit, someone who had inbuilt urges to destroy himself and those around him. But that can't be the whole, or even the most important part, of the story. The dark and angry stuff hurled from *The Holy Bible* came from deep within Richey Edwards's soul and it resonated with thousands of young people who bought the records and sang the songs.

The group sang about abortion ('Hitler reprised in the worm of your soul') and racism; they described the worship of beauty as conjured up in images of empty goddesses on pornographic magazine covers. They also entered the mysterious world of sadomasochism and sang about the glamorization of pain ('tear the torso with horses and chains, killers view themselves like they view the world; they pick at the holes, not punish less. Rise the pain, sterilize rapists, all I preach is extinction'). And they addressed uncomfortable subjects such as anorexia, bulimia and self-mutilation. The song entitled '4 stone 7 pounds' is startlingly honest. It describes a person suffering from anorexia whose stick-like limbs and sinking breasts are dramatic and very visual reminders of the gruesomeness of the disorder. The response of loved ones is predictable enough. A mother will want to find appetizing food for her suffering child. A father will look for excuses. But the person herself has a different outlook. She cares nothing for the horror of those who surround her. She finds self-worth, self-esteem, a bore. She's come to see an almost mystical dimension to her condition. She dreams of walking in the snow without leaving a footprint and finds 'such beautiful dignity in self-abuse'. Indeed, she claims to have discovered the meaning of life by letting her body waste away. 'Choice is skeletal', she announces. And the contemplation of the death of her body is where she begins to understand what life's all about.

This is a grim message and one easy response to it, as I've discovered scores of time when I've quoted it, is to suggest that it's just not typical of fun-chasing, life-loving, 'normal' young people. But that's to miss the point. These lyrics suggest the pose of a contemplative engaged in a deliberate search for meaning. Other voices, especially those of parents, intrude with their predictable and useless platitudes, but the predicament behind these words begs a multitude of questions of the empty, bleak, bankrupt institutions of conventional society. It's out of this same mish-mash of feelings that a character in the film of Irvine Welsh's book *Trainspotting* shouted out an observation he'd made. He'd noted how people wanted houses, how they took out mortgages, owned cars and fridges and all the consumer durables considered necessary. Then, with reference to one of Margaret Thatcher's most famous bons mots, he concluded his outburst with a great shout: 'There *is* such a thing as society,' he declared, '*and I want nothing to do with it.*'

Richey and the Manics gave expression to an alienation from basic values and a despair at prevailing norms that needed (and still need) to be heard and heeded. While the churches were preoccupied with homosexuality, sabbatarianism, gambling, contraception and the evils of cohabitation outside marriage; and while politicians were calling the nation 'back to basics'; while expensive holidays and exotic experiences, home improvements and the latest gadgetry, were opening up their own avenues in a hedonistic search for meaning; futility, emptiness, darkness were the only realities worth taking seriously by large numbers of young people. The agenda established by The Manic Street Preachers should be wrestled with by all who have an interest in an inclusive society. 'I cannot think of a single rock album from the past 25 years,' wrote one commentator, 'that occupies the same ground, the place where anger meets despair.' And, whatever else it is, this is intellectual soul-searching of the bleakest, most honest, kind.

James Bradfield offered an explanation for the efforts made by his group to speak to their generation. His words give good advice for anyone (and especially theologians) who might wish to deal with the intensely personal material buried within one's soul and make it accessible, universal. 'To be universal,' he said, 'you have got to stain the consciousness of the people. You've got to dig out a truth that everybody knows, but they don't want to hear, then tell it in a manner so aesthetically indignant, so beautiful, that they've got to accept it back into their lives again. That's what I want to do. Touch something universal with my own language.'

Another voice from this same general area has been that of Niall Griffiths whose two novels *Grits* (2000) and *Sheepshagger* (2001) have received widespread critical acclaim. The former is set in and around Aberystwyth, that erstwhile bastion of non-conformist piety, where a group of young drop-outs end up in each other's company. Through a series of monologues, each character sees the group and its activities from his or her own point of view and the combined effect of these brilliantly sustained efforts is to explore the deep fears and yearnings of the group and (we may suppose) their generation. It is hard and often unpleasant reading. The action is fuelled by alcohol, drugs, promiscuity and petty crime.

The bleak and dark contours of the countryside offer a perfect backdrop for the unfolding of the inner perspectives of these apparently amoral characters who despise the conventions of the society around them. Yet there's also an angry drive to question life, to probe for any meaning that may lurk somewhere within life's folds. Take this piece of reflection as an example:

> Even when you're feeling happy an content: a mean, well, wuv got, or if yerra Believer wuv been given, the capacity to experience an appreciate joy and rapture of and in this life, whether it's through drugs or sex or wharrever tickles yer fancy, an yet at the same time wuv also got the capacity to comprehend the complete extinction of such happiness, such joy! Wharrer sick fuckin joke![5]

We can enjoy or destroy. We can achieve these opposites as a consequence of our beliefs or else by enhancing our sensual responses through drugs or sex. At various times, one or another of the characters will try to explain just what drugs can and cannot deliver. For Malcolm, it is drugs that 'generate a defence against the vast blankness ahead, not just of death but also of the unknowable, unmapped future'. To Colm's mind, heroin helps to fill 'the void, the banality, the unbearable emptiness of everyday life'. Mairead reckons that it 'irons out your creases, counteracts your black energies, makes you horny, happy'. And she distinguishes between those drugs (like Ecstasy) that remove its users from reality, blanking out the real world, and alcohol, her own drug of choice, that 'whitewashes' the world, makes it foggy and opaque, but never takes it away completely. Whatever the exact understanding of their role, it's clear that drugs are considered essential for survival.

It is only in the world opened up by drugs and sex that there's any hope of finding meaning. None of the usual avenues lead anywhere. Mairead distinguishes her world from that of bank managers, bailiffs and 'those invisible forces' that shatter and then trample on other people's lives. Liam mocks the idea that anyone learns anything in universities. It's only once you get out of the lecture theatre and into the world that you can really learn. Colm spells it out even more clearly. Students, he observes, are all going to discover just how worthless a degree really is. Knowledge won't get anyone very far. In the end, life's not a matter of choosing what you most want to do but accepting what you don't want least.

Liam feels the same way about churches. Everything started to go wrong, he reckons, 'when they startud to build places whur we could supposedly meet God an ignore all the places whur ee actually is', out in the world. Sioned has much more mixed feelings about the Church, she recognizes that it does have something to offer, but, for the most part, the chapel is always there 'like a strict auntie, telling me off'. And she continues: 'It seems somehow that – in Wales – chapels and houses are arranged in such a way that no bedroom is ever free from the sight of a chapel – every bedroom looks out on a steeple – or part of one. It's always bloody there like. You can never get away from it.'[6] Even so, she'd dearly love to spit at the chapel at the end of her road.

In all this rejection and alienation, there are moments when values are identified and even hope expressed. These don't last long or come often but they stand out like nuggets in the bleak landscape. When Mairead had once told Colm that, compared with all the other men she'd been out with, he was 'the real thing', that he came across as the person he genuinely was, this affirmation had struck him as one of the best things that had ever happened to him. The sea, the hills, the breeze, the river – all can conspire to lift the heads of all of them towards some kind of inexpressible trans-cendence. Friendship matters and seems to have little to do with sex. Paul puts it succinctly when he suggests that the 'stuff that binds yuh together as probly got more tuh do with, erm, a dunno, recognizing somethin in others that either yuh want tuh see in yuhself or are too scared tuh see in yuhself; if anothuh person shows that quality, then yuh doan havter analyse it inside yuhself'. And Colm comes over quite coyly as he explains just why he'd enjoyed spend-ing time with a young woman in a pub. 'She was good to be with – talkin, lissenin, interested in me and my stories like . . . make me feel, a dunno, sort uv important a suppose.'

The dense, dark world of these drifters has little light in it, but there is, for all that, a yearning for beauty, meaning, warmth, relationships. These are not thought to be found in the institutions or conventions of society at large. These young people create their own society, no doubt hoping to find in the alternative culture of their own making, some of these elusive qualities and experiences. The outsider look-ing in can see how doomed they are, but their patent open-ness to what life might, just might, bring leaves a lingering sorrow and frustration that we've somehow shaped a soci-ety whose very achievements and decencies seem almost obscene to so many young people.

Niall Griffiths' second novel, *Sheepshagger*, is, if any-

thing, even bleaker. A group of friends act out their somewhat aimless lives helped along with a large and regular
intake of alcohol or drugs. One of their number, Ianto, is a
suppressed and mentally retarded member of the local community, object of fun much of the time and yet integrally a
member of the group. As described in the newspaper review
that led me to Griffiths' work, Ianto is 'a near-mute savant
with a mystical connection to nature who divides his time
between roaming the mountains of his childhood and
accepting whatever drink or drug is offered by his circle of
half-teasing, half-accepting friends.'[7] The story tells how he
found himself in a situation where forces were released
from his inmost being that led him to do unspeakable
deeds. He beats two people to death, two unsuspecting
people who cross his path while he's swept away by these
elemental forces. I've never read a more gruesome description of violence and death than here. The uncontrollable
rage that rises from within Ianto seems entirely in its place
against the backdrop of a pitiless tempest that sweeps
destructively across the hills and valleys of Wales. I had to
force myself to continue reading what was distinctly unpleasant stuff.

Right at the heart of this grim novel, almost at its mid-
point, a long discussion takes place between Ianto and his
friends. Tongues have been loosened by drink when Ianto's
friends notice a tick that had worked its way into his body
where it was filling itself with his blood. With a horrified
fascination (shared by the onlookers and readers alike) this
grim creature is removed and examined. What good do
creatures like this serve, one of Ianto's friends asks. What's
their place in the scheme of things? Why do they exist at all?
They're unpleasant and yet can hardly be blamed for the ill
they do. 'Evil', says Danny (the philosopher among them),
'is when you know the difference between right and wrong

and you still commit the wrongness for your own personal pleasure or gain. You know, like when you cause others to suffer cos their suffering will benefit you. That's evil.'

The tick just does what it needs to do in order to stay alive, he continues but that hardly constitutes evil. You have to look elsewhere for that. Then Danny reminisces: 'I remember when I was a kid, up at the chapel, and the vicar used to go on about how this world was made by a God who was all love and peace and understanding and that He wanted no harm to come to us, His favoured and best creation. And that we are all His children and He loves us all equally and without bounds and that if we loved Him back then when we died we'd go to Heaven and be with Him and all our dead relatives and live in eternal happiness for ever. And I remember thinking: what bollax. Complete fuckin shite. I mean if God loves us and cares for us then why does He make such things as phthisis and leeches and wasps? Germs and poisonous toadstools? Why does He send storms to blow our houses away? I mean one lad at the school died of a viper bite, seven years old and he dies of a viper bite. Why did God create a snake to kill that kiddie? Is that looking out for him to let him get bit by the adder?' When Danny asked the vicar, he was given an explanation wrapped up in the doctrine of original sin and details drawn from the story of Adam and Eve. Because of Adam's disobedience, the vicar argued, he put danger and evil within the world as a punishment. This all leads Danny to expostulate: 'If a force for good creates evil then evil wins.'

He then goes on to work this out. At the heart of the universe stands a supposedly all-powerful force that, whatever moral justification may be put forward, has, by creating evil, lost out to it. It's like a huge joke and leads to an order of existence where evil is rewarded and where good stands vulnerable and weak in its path. The only consolation for those who seek the good is that they will know their reward in the next world. This, says Danny, is plain daft; yet it's what the Church teaches, it's the very message 'spouted by people who are given great big houses to live in and positions of prominent power within local communities'.

In a universe that contains this mixture of good and evil, it's quite wrong to suppose that God is simply the force for good within it. He made it all and he *is* all of it. Preachers have got it all wrong. God can't be explained simply as 'pure good or love or peace or anything like that'. Nor merely the maker of the world. 'He *is* the world, this vast, this randomness.' No one knows when they turn the next corner whether they're going to meet a butterfly or an adder. Within an hour anyone could be dead or responsible for someone's death.

So then, asks one of the group, must we just resign ourselves to accept this mad world we live in? No, shouts Danny, and then draws his argument to a conclusion any preacher would be proud of. The world *is* a mad place, he concedes. It's much bigger than us and we can do nothing to change it. But for all that, we have to do what we can to make it 'saner, easier, to live in'. Surrounded by insanity, we simple have to search for peace. But this peace we all want is elusive; it's what we yearn for without even being able to give it a name. That's why we're all messed up. From the time we're born, we're caught up in the search for this peace (or whatever we'd call it) that could just make everything a little bit easier until the time comes for us to die. And all the while, the Church fobs us off with its talk of eternal bliss. It's as if the Church, seeking to perpetuate its own hold over people, deliberately avoids telling things as they really are, it refuses to spell out the hardness, the bleakness of life. 'God, heaven, sin, retribution . . . is all about a yearning, a need. It's about something we all want, something for us all to believe in.' Everyone needs to find a meaning to this life as well as cultivate a hope for the next one. If not, then everything's worthless and pointless.[8]

*Sheepshagger* is a difficult book but, once again (as with The Manic Street Preachers), it's hard to shake oneself free from the existential questions it raises. Niall Griffiths describes a grim world with the human lives within it pared down to the barest essentials. They fit well enough with the people Michel Foucault concerned himself with when he defined his 'limit experience'. These brutal novels certainly have their fair share of characters who seem to be perverts, criminals or the insane.

If Wales offers this bleak post-industrial, post-Christian, post-modern scene with no clear focus, a cultural and spiritual vacuum where discordant, alienated, counter-cultural voices endeavour to be heard, then there is one voice that has addressed this scene consistently throughout the whole period since the Second World War.

R. S. Thomas was a priest of the Church in Wales. I used to meet him in my Lampeter days; he'd come over from his parish in Eglwysfach. He certainly lived up to his reputation as a miserable old man. When he eventually allowed his autobiographies (there are three) to be translated into English, his true nature was revealed. He hated so much – the new liturgy of the Church, non-conformity in general, street lighting, cars and mechanization, the Irish (for letting their language go), nuclear weapons, the people of Chirk and Manafon and Eglwysfach (for not being 'Welsh' enough), the English and so on. He believed Wales was selling its soul, losing its language, abandoning its culture. 'Why, O why,' he wrote, 'doesn't the ordinary Welshman realize that the nation is fighting for its life? Does the anglicized Welshman who claims that he is as much of a Welshman as we, realize that he cannot even feel Welsh without falling back on the Welsh-language past? The fight for the language today is a fight for a future for the nation.' In other words, Thomas lined up with Saunders Lewis and the Welsh Language Society. As long ago as 1955, he'd written a poem that spoke of a Wales with only a past to celebrate. The future and the present meant little within a culture that was 'brittle with relics' and a people who'd become impotent through inbreeding, whose only joys seemed to spring from a maudlin fondness for singing old songs. It's as if the poet was seeking to accuse the nation of living up to its own stereotype while turning its back on its responsibilities.

He prophesied the collapse of the traditional, cultural and spiritual life of the nation. He saw all that clearly enough. Unfortunately, the only remedy he seemed able to identify for this state of affairs was the revival of the Welsh language. His negative attitude and joyless outlook hardly made him a likely choice to lead people towards the more meaningful life. He seems always to have hated life. He began his *Year in Llyn*, for example, with these words: 'This morning, I discovered the newborn year on my doorstep begging to be welcomed into the house. I hesitated for a moment for fear of what might come in its wake. But it continued to plead until I picked it up, not out of pity but because I had to.'

Yet Thomas wrote a corpus of poetry that spoke exactly to the state of his nation and, more widely than Wales, to a whole generation of people who, often (usually) dissatisfied with conventional institutions and traditional values, were searching for the very peace described by Danny in Niall Griffiths' novel. He is supremely the poet of darkness, the darkness of the human mind and the even worse darkness of the world around him. He describes this in his poem 'Threshold', where he suggests that the only thing to do when faced with such God-forsaken bleakness is, 'like

Michelangelo's Adam', to stretch one's hand into it all 'hoping for a reciprocating touch'.

Wherever Thomas introduces the notion of darkness, it is usually with a hint of the possibility of meaning or hope to be found at its heart. Indeed, it is only by committing oneself to the darkness that one can begin to search for any evidence that it is possessed of sustaining (rather than anni-hilating) qualities. It threatens to consume; but will it nec-essarily destroy? The 'reciprocating touch' of a hand held out in the dark can only be felt by risking the dark. In another poem, 'Alive', gazing out into an impenetrable night, the poet declares that 'the darkness is the deepening shadow of your presence'. Elsewhere ('Silence'), he describes human beings as wanderers 'in the darkness that was never a long way off from his presence'. The darkness of God's countenance as described in 'Counterpoint' is set alongside 'the luminosity of his shadow', and the human predicament is compared in a poem called 'Citizen' to walk-ing along a 'shining tightrope between dark and dark' where the best we can manage is just 'one step forward and one back'.

The pilgrim's way may well be strung between a long-obscured point of departure and a not-yet-in-view place of arrival. The 'fixed points' (Where do I come from? and Where am I going?) are shrouded in darkness. It's in the travelling alone that hope continues to shine. This paradox is developed again and again by Thomas. In a poem called 'Shadows', for example, he imagines himself closing his eyes and finding within his mind a darkness that, far from being oppressive, seems pregnant with the sense of the presence of God. It's as if his own internal darkness was in reality the shadow cast across it by the 'steep mind' of God. This possibility sends a shiver down his back and leads him to conclude that we human beings should not expect to be blinded by God's light so much as to be surprised by the 'splendour of [his] darkness'.

Again and again, Thomas makes it clear that darkness is somehow invested with the light of God's presence. The paradox is indeed stark, but it seems to speak a language that the well-read Manic Street Preachers and the characters in Niall Griffiths' novels would warm to rather more than the conventional language of the Church that they seem to rail against. Darkness, for Thomas, far from being a cloak for nothingness, meaninglessness, the annihilation of the self, turns out to be charged with intimations of the mysterious presence of the living God.

The poet also develops the idea of the God who remains hidden from view, the absent God, *deus absconditus*. In 'The Prisoner', for example, he refers directly to this idea, suggesting that when 'we ransack the heavens, the distance between stars', all we discover is that God is not there. In his poem 'Adjustments', Thomas goes even further. 'Never known as anything but an absence,' he writes, 'I dare not name him as God.' In 'The Possession', meanwhile, a religious man looks around with worried eyes 'at the emptiness' around him. He looks out at the lights of a big city, for example, and concludes that for all the brilliance there's nobody there! Then he concludes his meditation in typical style with the recognition that all he can claim to have is the tiniest understanding of 'the universal mind that reflects infinite darkness between points of light'.

Darkness hides the face of God and we have to live with the fact of his hiddenness, but we do not need to confront such realities in a state of hopelessness. Thomas' absent God seems somehow different from the divine being of those mystics who trod the *via negativa*, the negative way. His God, though absent, seems still close at hand. How else do we understand his poem called 'The Absence', which describes God with one paradox after another? He is a 'great absence' who, for all that, feels just like 'a presence'. He's a being who, while he expects to be addressed, gives little hope of a reply. He remains elusive; seeking to encounter him feels just like entering a room 'from which someone has just gone'.

Sometimes, argues the poet, we find ourselves poised on the edge of a moment of discovery and, losing our footing, we fall 'into a presence illimitable as its absence, descending motionlessly in space-time, not into darkness but into the luminosity of his shadow' ('Counterpoint'). It's all so frustrating that absence should suggest presence and yet, at the same time, exclude us from holding on to anything we can recognize. Such a God leaves us hanging on to a distant view of his coat tails, rarely blessed with much more than the merest hint of his presence. No wonder it all leaves us either filled with a sense of awe, or else empty of any sense at all of God's being. He seems to play hide-and-seek with us. We look beyond ourselves and he is not there. We search within and discover that he's not there either. And yet we feel compelled to continue the search because we never succeed in ridding ourselves of the idea of his existence. As Thomas puts it in 'Counterpoint', 'everywhere there is confetti, but there are no vows kept'.

Thomas conveys the frustration he feels often enough but he never dips into despair. For even though God may seem not to be there when we turn, yet he is somehow there 'in the turning'. Thomas' poetry is filled with pictures of the reaching out of faith to God, something done in the spirit of hoping against hope, with arms stretched out into a deep darkness. It is bleak, spare stuff. It has little of the bland or the sugary. It speaks to the spiritual condition of so many modern (and post-modern) people. We live at a time when the brutality of human beings has inflicted untold pain and suffering on millions; where the greed of human beings has raped the fair earth and left its violated body poised between life and death. God has been pushed to the margins, dispossessed of his own home. The absence of God is a very real experience for so many. Thomas somehow keeps alive the possibility of presence-in-absence. This counterpoint is exquisitely conveyed in his 'Via Negativa' where, even after admitting to himself that he senses God as a 'great absence' and an 'empty silence', he refuses to give up the search for someone who seems to inhabit 'the interstices in our knowledge' and 'the darkness between stars'. Faith becomes a matter of listening for echoes of a voice we never hear directly, or following the footprints of someone we never catch up with. When we look at other people, we may well suspect that he has looked at them too and yet, for all that, we fail to see his reflection in them. The search has to go on. It's an endless journey. A pilgrimage of hoping against hope.

The mystery of God is so deep and we can so easily trivialize him with our piety. The profundity of the darkness and the desolation of the absence conspire to make us feel just how little we are, how pathetic our attempts in liturgy, prayer or devotion to get anywhere near the Great Mystery who is God. The bankruptcy of non-conformity, an ineffectual Church in Wales, a 'foreign' Roman Catholicism (riven these days by sexual scandal), have lost hold on the population of the principality. They've all been shaken to the core. It's the Church in Wales, by recymricizing itself, that seems best placed to rise phoenix-like from the ashes. It alone seems to have the capacity to become an inclusive body and to reach out to a whole people.

Meanwhile, a number of fantasies are still being played out by various sectors of a society still in denial. There are those who suppose, for example, that the salvation of

Wales is somehow exclusively dependent upon the health of the Welsh language. Others are working on the assumption that free churches who, throughout their history have stood aloof from each other, can now weather the storms of unbelief and the flight from organized religion by joining together and entering some kind of redoubt, a Custer's last stand, in their battle against the erosion of faith. And then there are those, within Wales and beyond it, who seem to believe that a magic potion can somehow be found in what is called generically 'Celtic Spirituality'. On close examination, of course, so much of this turns out to be little more than a haphazard collection of old nostrums and doggerel, a pot pourri of verse and worse put together hurriedly to meet the insatiable demands of the 'body, mind and spirit' market. And that leaves despair, the kind of utter hopelessness (bordering on nihilism) shown by characters in Niall Griffiths' novels.

The poetry of R. S. Thomas offers a spirituality for dark and messy times. We now need a theology to match it.

---

## Questions for discussion

1. How does the Church avoid becoming a judgmental, moralistic community?

2. Could The Manic Street Preachers be latter-day prophets?

3. Have you experienced a bleakness as intense as that described in the novels of Niall Griffiths? Just how do we recognize the existence (or the possibility) of hope amid such despair?

4. How does the poetry of R. S. Thomas help to shape a spirituality for our (messy) times?

# 4

# In the parish of the poor: the wretched story of Haiti

In August 1970, newly married, my wife and I arrived in Port-au-Prince, capital city of the Caribbean Republic of Haiti. We were to spend the greater part of the next ten years there. This period of my life and my encounter with the people of this poor country have undoubtedly given me more understanding of the world we live in than any other experience I've ever had. Let me explain.

I was stationed in Petit Goâve, a country town 30 dusty miles away from the capital. I was given responsibility for 48 churches, the furthest of which was a 24-hour mule ride away from home. A number of these could only be visited by taking a seven-hour boat trip across to an island called La Gonâve. I've often thought subsequently that my responsibility for these far-flung places made me a bishop before I was ever ordained!

Haiti's official language is French. Indeed, it's because I could get by reasonably well in it that I'd been sent there. I was soon to discover that hardly anyone there speaks it! They use the local Créole language that, while it shares an extensive vocabulary with French, remains structurally as different from it as can be. My own command of this local tongue was nil. I'd come to Haiti confident of my ability to bring hope and comfort to the poor. I was well-qualified and full of cheerful optimism. Suddenly I found myself totally de-skilled and disempowered. I couldn't utter a word without help. In this situation of utter dependency, it was the peasant people of Haiti who took me in hand. They taught me their language and the secrets of their culture, they shared their wit and their wisdom, they opened their hearts and their homes. They were patient with me and generous to a fault. Thus I became useful and thus I was always afterwards to see the affairs of Haiti through the eyes of its peasant population rather than, more conventionally, through those of the city-dwelling political class.

Haiti is the poorest country in the Western world. Life expectancy is low, child mortality, unemployment, illiteracy are all sky high. The people are malnourished but somehow survive and, wonder of wonders, do so with flair. Their music and their art, their proverbs and their folktales, all offer powerful evidence of a rich culture and an indomitable spirit. When I arrived among them I was an arrogant brat. My education had put a veneer on me, a kind of gloss, that separated me from the poor and vulnerable person I'd once been. It had given me social skills and a passport to the world of employment and wealth, but only at a cost, only by denying (or at least hiding) the person I'd been. It was Haiti that put the two halves of my divided self back together again. By stripping me right down to the barest essentials, robbing me of the more superficial benefits won by my education, I was put back in touch with my humble beginnings and my deepest self. The people of Haiti, who have so little, in Western terms, healed me. They did what all the king's horses and all the king's men were manifestly unable to do for Humpty Dumpty – they put me back together again. However mawkish it seems, I must pay tribute in this way to one of the most misunderstood and ill-appreciated peoples on the face of the planet. I shall be forever in their debt.

There were two larger-than-life phenomena awaiting us when we arrived there in 1970. One was the dictatorship of Dr François Duvalier. The other was the presence on the ground of liberation theology. These might be expected to pull in opposite directions; they are, after all, poles apart. One was inflicting all kinds of terror on the people of Haiti while the other, harnessing energies released by the recently concluded Vatican Council, sought nothing more than the release of the people from the forces that had oppressed them for far too long. And yet, for all this appearance of radical difference, I was to make the startling discovery that 'PapaDoc' Duvalier and the liberation theologians had a great deal in common. Indeed, both were the issue of the same social forces and an expression of a deep popular yearning to turn Haitian society upside-down. Such a strange comparison needs a careful explanation. It also needs a little knowledge of Haiti's colourful and eventful history.

Very few people know much about the history of this, the first black republic in the world. Nor, on the whole, do they care to know more. We prefer to make our judgements on the basis of current events. A massacre is self-evidently a bad thing and maintaining power through the sanctioned use of a secret police network is obviously anti-democratic. So why bother with history? The truth is clear. The dictator should be held up for the wicked man he is. His deeds speak for themselves and, anyway, they make far better copy than boring lessons about the past. The past can't rescue the present from the atrocities it groans under.

Yet I plead for a more considered approach. Listening to voices from this desert might be difficult but, for all that, needs to be attempted.

When we arrived there in Haiti in 1970, Duvalier was nearing the end of his 14-year reign. I'd read Graham Greene's *The Comedians* and had followed avidly the latest newspaper reports of the dreadful repression imposed on the Haitian people by its sinister and ghoulish president. Just before we travelled, Bernard Diederich and Al Burt brought out their *Papa Doc: Haiti and its Dictator,* a searing indictment of the dictator and his infamous secret police (the 'Tontons Macoute').[1] I swallowed the myth hook, line and sinker and accepted the received wisdom that told me we were going to a hellish place. I expected to be in for a hard ride.

The following ten years were to challenge those first impressions and to open my eyes to the way the 'world order' we live in relegates countries like Haiti to the very margins of life. The economic and political structures within which we in the Western world live seem, somehow, to need to keep the poorest nations of the world on the edge of survival as if this, and only this, can keep them 'safe for democracy'. I'm convinced that such has been the experience of Haiti over the 200 years of its independent history. And it was a reaction to these forces that first brought 'PapaDoc' Duvalier on to the political stage. He came to power as the champion of the poor. Only later did he turn into the monster he became. I feel these days as if I want to justify, or at least offer a reasoned statement for, one of the most notorious despots of his time. He was by no means a one-dimensional cardboard cut-out figure; rather, he was a complex character whose case needs to be heard at the bar of history.

In July 1915, the USS Washington steamed into the Port-au-Prince harbour to begin an occupation by the American marines that would continue until 1934. By that time, Haiti's reputation was already well and truly sealed. Its heroic birth in 1804, achieved against the might of an army led by Napoleon Bonaparte's brother-in-law (General Leclerc), had come about without the skilled presence of a midwife. Isolated from the world of slave-owning powers whose colonies lay all around it, it had to find its way forward as best it could. No one should have been surprised that it resorted to militaristic or monarchical 'top down' modes of governance. That was all they'd known and no one was helping them to develop anything else. Even Simon Bolivar, who'd been given material assistance by one of Haiti's first presidents at the outset of his liberating mission to Central and South America, colluded with a racist world order by attending a pan-American meeting of the newly independent nations of the region in 1825 that specifically excluded Haiti. The president of the United States in those antebellum days refused to sit down with a black head of state, and Bolivar went along with that arbitrary decision, to the eternal shame of this great freedom fighter.

Recognition for independent Haiti came only slowly and very reluctantly, starting in the late 1820s and culminating only in the 1860s when the Vatican and Washington finally came on board. In the case of the Roman Catholic Church, it needed major concessions on the part of the Haitian government even then. Rome maintained the absolute right to choose and appoint bishops for Haiti and in this way kept a stranglehold on the church there that was to last until the time of Duvalier. As for the United States, it took a civil war and the ending of slavery before they found it possible to recognize the black leadership of Haiti.

Things went from bad to worse. A book written in 1874 by a British diplomat, Spenser St John's *Hayti or the Black Republic*, changed perceptions of the land of Toussaint Louverture forever. To the public mind, this place that had always been faintly ridiculous and irrelevant now became a land of wickedness and black magic. The book focused on a show trial where eight poor peasants were accused of having committed cannibalistic acts while practising the dark arts of voodoo. The Haitian government of the time was pursuing this trial in order to prove to the outside world that it could deal with its 'pagan' and 'backward' elements in order to claim its proper place among the civilized nations of the modern world. In fact, it achieved precisely the opposite. St John's presence throughout the trial (together with his American, French and Spanish confrères), resulted in descriptions of Haiti as a benighted, ghoulish and evil society being relayed back to their respective governments. The reputation gained by Haiti at that time has never really changed.

That is certainly the way things were in American eyes when they began their military occupation. A Haitian president had been deposed and murdered in the early part of 1915 and this became the pretext for the invasion. The US marines, they claimed, were coming to restore stability and to bring order out of chaos. It was useless to protest that if a presidential assassination could be taken as a sufficient reason to invade another country then the Americans, who'd experienced three such assassinations in the previous half century, might be particularly susceptible! Nor did anyone ask if the real reason for invading Haiti (as well as other nearby countries) might have had something to do with protecting the approaches to the recently opened Panama Canal.

In the first months of the occupation, a new constitution was written. This was the work of the Assistant Secretary of State for the Navy, none other than the young Franklin D. Roosevelt. There had been a number of versions of the constitution since 1804; each differed on points of detail, to reflect the political agenda of the time, but they all subscribed to one article of faith. They each opened with the statement that Haiti belonged to its people and that no foreigner would be allowed to buy or own land there. The American rewrite of the Haitian constitution promptly reversed this clause and a carefully orchestrated plebiscite was held to give a show of support for the new arrangements. With almost indecent haste, large tracts of land were bought up by US companies and sugar, sisal, fruit and minerals were developed and fat profits expatriated. Puppet governments were installed, the Haitian army reorganized and its officers trained in the United States, an intelligence service (reporting to Washington) set up and the Haitian national debt removed from the Paris Bourse in favour of Wall Street. Substantial capital projects of arguable usefulness to the Haitian people (a railway line, for example) were launched with little local consultation. In a very short space of time, Haiti was turned from a struggling but independent nation into an American vassal state. Through all of this, its rural populations, scratching a living from subsistence farming, were completely marginalized.

Huge resentments were being created through these years. A young Haitian named Charlemagne Péralte mounted an armed resistance to the occupation. He was instantly considered to be a 'terrorist' and hunt-and-kill groups of marines fanned out over the countryside in search of him and his supporters. When he was eventually tracked down and killed, his body was brought back to Port-au-Prince strapped to a door that had been removed for the purpose. His posture bore an uncanny resemblance to a crucifixion and photographic images of the dead man were soon circulating far and wide, an icon for a people yearning for their old freedoms.

The Americans remained until 1934. The first and only visit of a US President saw the same Franklin D. Roosevelt who had set Haiti's descent into a vassal state into motion return to sign the treaty of disengagement. Yet the political, commercial and social influence of Haiti's northern neighbour continued to be overwhelming.

One ironic consequence of the American occupation, a direct consequence of the presence of the white occupier, was the arousal of a great deal of interest in the African roots of Haitian life and culture. This came about partly through the work of foreign ethnologists and sociologists. *Life in a Haitian Valley*, for example, was published by Melville J. Herskovits in 1937[2] and James G. Leyburn's *The Haitian People* appeared four years later.[3] These books, very detailed and carefully written, were the work of American scholars who had conducted field work in rural Haiti in the mid-1930s and represented a serious effort on the part of established academics to understand Haiti. They certainly offered a radical contrast to Spenser St John's sensationalism. And this tone was maintained by the Trinidadian historian C. L. R. James whose brilliant book *The Black Jacobins* came out in 1938 and told the tale of the heroism of a slave population whose victory over the French represents one of the greatest military surprises of all time. Books like these focused on Haiti's African roots. They brought the Haitian peasant centre stage. Previously, as part of the effort to bring Haiti to the attention of the international community, it had been customary to dwell on its French antecedents.

Underlying these efforts by foreigners was a prodigious amount of work undertaken by Haitians themselves. The 'indigenous movement' was pioneered by one of the greatest of all Haitian intellectuals, Jean Price-Mars. He published his seminal study of Haitian ethnography and folklore, *Ainsi Parla l'Oncle* ('This is what the Old Man said'),[4] in 1927 and his work was a major contribution to the creation of a national identity after a dozen years of the American occupation. And hard at work in this same endeavour was a young doctor of medicine, François Duvalier. Through the early 1940s, he worked with a team of American medical experts in the campaign against a tropical disease known as yaws. This had given him a close relationship with the Americans, but, far more important, it gave him an even closer familiarity with the Haitian peasantry. This was to mark him for life. He became aware of the heaving rural masses, people normally overlooked by those directing the nation's affairs. Their plight moved him deeply as did their potential to change the political configuration of Haiti if only their latent energy could be harnessed. This was precisely the sentiment contained in a poem by one of Duvalier's friends, Carl Brouard, entitled 'Vous' (You).

> You,
> the rabble,
> the filthy,
> the stinking:
> peasant women coming down from our hills,
> baby in belly,
> horny old men, toilers on the land,
> feet drilled by vermin,
> whores,
> and you,
> the decrepit, dragging yourselves along
> in the stench of your wounds, thick with flies.
>
> You,
> all of you common people,
> stand up!
> Now for the clean sweep.

You are the pillars of society,
you get out
and it all collapses, like a house of cards.

Then, then,
you will know you are a tidal wave
whose power remains hidden.

Wave!
Gather yourself,
boil up,
roar,
till under your shroud of foam,
nothing remains, nothing
but what is clean through and through,
scoured, well washed,
bleached right down to the bone.

These words were written in 1927 and appeared in a journal called *La Revue Indigéniste* (The Indigenous Review). Duvalier worked hard within a movement that shone the spotlight, almost for the first time in Haiti's independent history, on the peasant population and on the African origins of much that constituted Haitian culture. By far his most interesting book *Le problème des classes à travers l'histoire d'Haïti* (The Class Problem in Haitian History) was published while in government in the years following the withdrawal of the Americans. In it, Duvalier analysed the struggle for power between his country's mulattos and blacks, a struggle dating back to the very beginnings of Haitian history. It was the mulattos who, on the whole, had won out by currying favour first with the French and then with the Americans. He watched their manoeuvrings from close at hand. The arrangements that kept Haiti sweet for the Americans led to substantial wealth accruing to a very

small minority of families within Haiti. The rural populations, meanwhile, tended to live outside the organized
economy and in desperate poverty.

When Duvalier won the 1957 presidential election, he
caught everyone by surprise. The Americans had wanted a
different result but, since Duvalier had worked with them
in his days as a doctor, they assumed he would be pliable
enough. So they welcomed the outcome though adding
caution. Duvalier had seen the capacity of the United States
to make and unmake governments in Haiti and he had no
difficulty recognizing his need to keep Washington happy
with his performance, but he found himself up against
formidable opposition at home.

The national army set him his first challenge. It had been
set up to be a tool for keeping Haiti firmly pro-American.
Its top command consisted mainly of mulatto officers,
many of them members of one of the leading families in
Haiti's commercial life. Duvalier was black and wanted to
bring new people into Haiti's economic mainstream but he
knew he'd soon come up against opposition from the
armed forces. He knew too that he'd have to master that
institution if he wanted freedom to act. He soon removed
all the old brigade and replaced them with officers of his
own choosing. When they rebelled against his decrees, he
took severe measures against them including stringing up a
number of them in a public execution in one of Port-au-
Prince's major thoroughfares. He left their decaying
corpses hanging there for several days as a public reminder
of who was in charge. Soon, he added insult to injury by
establishing the Tontons Macoutes, his own secret police.
This was never a paid force, they were strictly speaking
volunteers but, armed with a gun, they were given freedom
to proceed as they wished. No one would ask questions
about any action or personal enrichment they enjoyed as a

result of their nefarious activities. Their only loyalty, and this was to be absolute, was to Duvalier himself. They were to be his eyes and ears.

Within a couple of years, Duvalier had negated the power of the press, the business community and the army. He'd done this despite American unease and had been helped immeasurably by the success of Fidel Castro's invasion against the pro-American Battista régime in neighbouring Cuba. Duvalier played this card very deftly. Washington now needed Haiti's support in its obsessive struggle against international communism. They would now be prepared to turn a blind eye to much of what Duvalier got up to. He didn't waste his opportunity. After a tentative start, his transformation into an absolute dictator became more and more inevitable.

There was one other institution to be combated, however, and that was the Church. Since the 1860 Concordat, a succession of Breton or Canadian bishops had exercised a stranglehold on Haiti's religious life. In a century of total control, there had been almost no Haitian candidates for the priesthood. The Church had charge of significant areas of Haitian life. It educated the children of the elite, it ran their hospitals, and it shaped their minds. In Duvalier's view, it amounted to a state within the state and was accountable to powers beyond Haiti's shores. This was unacceptable to him. He expelled the Jesuits and, later, most of the bishops. The Vatican responded by excommunicating him.

At this point the most extraordinary concurrence of events virtually gave Duvalier everything he wanted. One of the decisions of the Second Vatican Council had been to indigenize local churches. The liturgy was being vernacularized and, all over the world, the search was on within national churches for leaders able to take the community of

faith into its new chapter of history. Since Duvalier's own
declared aim was to bring the Roman Catholic Church in
Haiti under the control of local bishops, observers were
soon noting that he and the Vatican were now seeking an
identical objective. Negotiations began and Duvalier's
version of what happened next is contained in a remarkable
piece of propaganda, a book entitled *Mémoires d'un leader
du Tiers Monde* (Memories of a Third World Leader) in
which he tells the world how he drove the discussions
towards his desired goal. It certainly led to the almost
immediate appointment of three Haitian bishops, including
Mgr Wolff Ligondé as Archbishop of Port-au-Prince. It also
led to a very Erastian phase in Haitian church life that saw
bishops dancing dutifully to Duvalier's tune. They gave the
increasingly barbarous dictator an air of legitimacy and
even morality.

The rest of the story of François Duvalier need not be
rehearsed here. The effort needed to secure his power base
reduced him to paranoia and turned Haiti into a police state.
People will always argue whether or not he really intended
to reconfigure Haiti's political agenda in order to give the
rural masses a greater participation in national life. He was
certainly trusted by them and knew exactly how to appeal
to them for support. He used the Créole language judi-
ciously and seemed to understand the place of the voodoo
religion in their lives. In the end, however, he did little for
them and his dire deeds fully earned him his reputation as
one of his generation's most ruthless and brutal dictators.

This has been a long narrative where I've tried to explain
how Duvalier came to power in 1957 with a unique knowledge and experience of all the factors that had reduced his
country to the level of total subservience to a foreign power.
He'd been closely allied to a number of intellectuals who,
by concentrating their attention on Haiti's Africanness, had

prepared the case for a new nationalism to combat the puppet rulers content to take their orders from Washington, but he couldn't turn this concern into political action when given the chance to do so. He never felt able to relax long enough to give his attention to his political objectives. Paranoia set in and the rest is history. Meanwhile, the peasant people of Haiti, went on much as before. From their point of view, they'd been sold down the river yet again.

It was 20 years after Duvalier's death in 1971 before the next ray of hope shone on Haiti's poor. During that period, Jean-Claude Duvalier had overseen a period of increasing decadence and corruption before he was finally ousted in 1986. He was followed by a succession of military governments whose only common factor was their incompetence. And then, with the collapse of communism and the end of the Cold War, the international community became increasingly unhappy with regimes they'd put up with for years. Now 'accountable government' became a requirement and 'democratization' the buzzword on everybody's lips. And so the old anti-democratic order that had come into existence to serve the needs of the Great Powers now had to give way to something more transparent, again to suit the changing expectations (and fashions) of the world community.

Haiti was no exception to this rule but there was something unique happening there. The new world order happened to come at the very time when energies long latent in Haiti were being released. A quiet revolution was in the making and it centred around one man – Jean-Bertrand Aristide.

Aristide was a Roman Catholic priest who, having shown brilliance at school, was favoured by the Salesian Order for an extensive formation undertaken in several countries and across a number of disciplines. He was already a voracious reader when the first fruits of liberation theology began tumbling from the press.

It was the Second Vatican Council's 'Pastoral Constitution on the Church in the Modern World' (*Gaudium et Spes*) that opened the way for what would become liberation theology. The Council had closed in December 1965 and soon regional conferences of bishops were being held to discuss and apply its findings. The second such conference in Latin America took place in Medellin in Colombia in 1968 and it formulated its now-famous 'preferential option for the poor'. It also described the poverty and injustice that prevailed on the continent as 'those realities that constitute a sinful situation'. Sin was thus defined in more than a mere personal sense, it acquired an institutional and structural dimension too. This corporate and systemic way of thinking about the nature of evil soon became central to the thinking of the first generation of liberation theologians.

This work was undertaken by the Uruguayan Jesuit Juan Luis Segundo, the Peruvian Gustavo Gutiérrez, Jon Sobrino (a Basque Jesuit working in El Salvador) and the Brazilian Franciscan Leonardo Boff. When Gutiérrez's book *A Theology of Liberation* was published in 1971, it became the most influential publication of its type and canonized the use of the label 'liberation theology'.

Liberation theologians work hand in glove with colleagues in the social sciences, economics, history and political theory. This interdisciplinary approach allows them to get to grips with the world in which people actually live and also to work out the moral consequences of a faith that seeks to respond to social oppression within that world. But the very first objective of this school of theology is to raise the awareness of those who suffer from exploitation and injustice. The inelegant word for this is 'conscientization.' As this process occurs, so those who begin to recognize the forces that oppress them are likely to want to confront those forces. People marginalized by the system now seek inclusion within it and are prepared, if necessary, to resort to direct action to achieve it. The theology of liberation presupposes the liberation of theology. Until theology ceases to identify with the values, interests and goals of those who benefit from structural injustice, then theology can have nothing to contribute to the liberation movement.

All of this was being worked out in Haiti in the 1970s by groups of priests working deep in the countryside. By 1982, this had developed to the point where a grassroots movement was officially launched within the church. It was called *Ti Kominote Legliz*, (literally 'little church communities', a more pleasing tag than the customary 'ecclesial base communities'), a title that soon gave way to the simpler *Ti Legliz*, (the Little Church). Small groups of lay Christians began to meet across the length and breadth of the republic to address questions that related the gospel to the social realities around them. This was liberation theology at its purest and simplest and it was present in Haiti long before the return of Jean-Bertrand Aristide after the completion of his studies. These groups encouraged lay people to claim their rights and urged them forward to play a part in Haiti's political life. This was a startling development. These were people who'd never taken an active part in public affairs before. Soon the unrest stirred up by these activities became insistent. The government began to be worried by what was happening and, in December 1982, arrested some of the leaders of the *Ti Legliz*. But the people were expecting the authorities to respond in this way. They took to the streets and, as a result of sustained and concerted pressure, with the active leadership of the Church collaborating fully, they succeeded in securing the release of those who'd been arrested. This was a very significant reversal for those in power, it was a warning shot across the bows of the government of that time.

Aristide was still abroad pursuing his studies when Pope John Paul II made his fleeting visit to Haiti in March 1983. The repercussions of that visit were considerable. At a mass held on the runway of the international airport, he delivered a speech in the Créole language. This pope, who had criticized priests who got themselves involved in politics, delivered a sermon that galvanized all the progressive forces in the land, even the bishops and the papal nuncio, for the last throes of the struggle against the Duvalier regime. 'There must be a better distribution of goods,' Pope John Paul declaimed, 'and a fairer organization of society with more popular participation in its affairs and a more generous concept of service on the part of those who direct society.' This was radical enough but he hadn't finished: 'I appeal to all those who have power, wealth and culture, to understand their urgent responsibility towards all their brothers and sisters.' And then he finished with a stirring rallying cry. 'Things must change here', he thundered.

The whole church took the pope at his word. For a brief moment, bishops and archbishops became liberation theologians. They published document after document calling the country to action. One of these quoted the 1968 Medellin Conference and set out a very clear agenda for change. It pointed out that politics has a global dimension since it envisages the common good. The definition of Haiti's needs must not be left to political scientists alone. On the contrary, the duty to protect the basic human rights of all members of society and to defend the peasant population against the illegal seizing of their property (especially their land) belongs to everyone. The document went on to condemn the violation of the justice system, the use of torture, arbitrary arrest and illegal detention.

All this was heady stuff. Soon the whole country was in a ferment. By February 1986, the game was up for Jean-Claude Duvalier. He and his entourage left the country under cover of night never to return. The next five years saw a succession of repressive military governments. It proved to be a very difficult time for everyone and the leadership of the Roman Catholic Church, having shown such courage and imagination in their efforts to depose the dictator, now began to have cold feet. They failed to follow through with the very plans they had only recently announced. A universal literacy campaign was abandoned and many other initiatives became stalled.

Aristide's reaction was predictable enough. He railed not only against those holding the levers of political power but also his own superiors in the Church. There were several attempts on his life and many twists and turns in his own development as he moved from his life as a priest to his responsibilities in the political sphere. In the end, he stood as a candidate in the December 1990 election and was returned as president with a massive 67 per cent share of the vote.

In 1990, a collection of Aristide's writings appeared in print. It was called *In the Parish of the Poor* and gives a flavour of sermons and talks he gave during his ministry in the slum parish of Don Bosco in downtown Port-au-Prince. People flocked to hear him. He combined an otherworldly mysticism with some very this-worldly analysis. He spoke in parables and forged an extraordinary bonding with his hearers. His sermons became events. They exuded the spirit of prophecy. He seemed to become a vehicle through whom God's own voice spoke.

In November 1988, Aristide spoke on one of Haiti's radio stations. One military government had just succeeded another to the widespread dissatisfaction of the people.

There had been a general strike and Aristide had been near the centre of everything that was happening. Indeed, he was becoming a focal point for the opposition to military rule that was mounting daily. His links with his religious order, the Salesians, were getting more and more tenuous as he continued his attacks not only the military but also on the Church. His broadcast talk was in Créole. It was a masterpiece of its type.

> To my sisters, my brothers,
> To all my brothers and sisters in the Good Lord
> Who raise their voices together with us,
> To the valiant youth of Haiti,
> To the peasants – whether Catholic, Protestant, or
>     Vodouisant,
> To the brave Haitians abroad,
> To the courageous Haitians here in Haiti,
> And to all of you who have just achieved a legal general
>     strike
> In spite of the declarations of an illegal General:
> Hats off to you,
> Congratulations on your courage.

People gathered round their radios roared with appreciative laughter at the saucy play on words that contrasted the 'legal general strike' with the 'illegal General' at the head of government. Aristide went on to repeat his admiration for the people's courage and to assure them that he saw God in what they were doing, that he heard God's voice in their voice. He continued:

> A beautiful inspiration from the Holy Spirit!
> A beautiful declaration of brotherly love, a declaration
> Which invites me to look you in the eye, my sisters and
>     brothers,

And to say to you what Jesus would have said to you
In his language: *Ani ohev otha, ani ohev ota'kh*.
I love you.

There was widespread admiration and approval at his use
of this Aramaic quotation. So many of his followers were
illiterate but they took real pleasure in knowing that their
champion could hold his own in half a dozen living
languages to say nothing of the three dead ones he'd also
mastered. At this point the orator moves into a different
gear. He accuses three bishops and also the papal nuncio *by
name* and blames them for plotting against him and the
Haitian people. 'Let me look you in the eye,' he pleads with
them. 'Don't be ashamed,' he goads, 'look me in the eye.'

I've come to tell you: I love you too.
Because I love you, I must tell you the truth.
Truth and love are the same.
Truth and love are Jesus in the midst of the poor.

This ironic chastisement of bishops and archbishops by
one of their priests won the approval of the people but it
drove nails into Aristide's coffin. They wouldn't forget this
humiliation in a hurry. But he hadn't finished with them
yet:

What luck for the Haitian Church,
Rich, thanks to the poor,
In a country that is poor because of the rich.
The Church is rich thanks to us, the poor
Who ceaselessly demand the truth
From every corner.

He develops the motifs 'rich thanks to the poor' and
'poor because of the rich', building them into a litany of
accusation aimed at the Church, the army high command

(he was always careful to honour the junior ranks), the business community and former Duvalierists. Then, in echoes of Carl Brouard's poem quoted earlier in this chapter, he introduces the metaphor of the flood. This was to become one of his key themes in the run up to the election and continues to be the name borne by his political party to this day. Elements of this next passage became his rallying cry on the hustings and at all his public meetings:

Alone, we are weak.
Together, we are strong.
All together, we are the flood.

Let the flood descend, the flood of
Poor peasants and poor soldiers,
The flood of the poor jobless multitudes (and poor
    soldiers),
Of poor workers (and poor soldiers),
The flood of all our poor friends (and all the poor
    soldiers) and
The church of the poor, which we call the children
    of God!
Let that flood descend!
And then God will descend and put down the mighty
    and send them away,
And he will raise up the lowly and place them on high.

To prevent the flood of the children of God from
    descending,
The imperialists in their cassocks have conspired with
    the imperialists in America.
This is why we Haitians must say to one another what
    Jesus declared:
Arise! Go forth! Walk! . . .

Too much blood has been spilled!
Too many of the innocent have fallen!
This is too much for us.[5]

It is quite difficult to convey a sense of the immediacy and
power of this utterance or the direct accusations of named
individuals with which it closed. This was what made
Aristide such a dangerous man to contend with. The sym-
biosis between him and the poor people of Haiti was total.
Indeed, in another of his rallying calls, he declared that the
Haitian people and he were twins. They were inseparable
from each other. They belonged together.

I've tried to describe and assess the power of Aristide's
oratory elsewhere. This is what I wrote in 1994:

Imagine a litany that runs like this. The diminutive priest,
raised up on a distant platform, would intone one word
into his microphone. '*Apart*' ('On our own'), he'd say,
and then the crowd, as one, would reply '*nou fèb*' ('we're
weak'). '*Ansanm*' ('together'), he'd continue, to which
'*nou fo*' ('we're strong'), they'd cry, much louder this
time. '*Ansanm ansanm*' ('and when we're **all** together'),
he'd insist, '*nou se lavalas*' ('we're the flood') they'd hurl
back with relish, their voices themselves a veritable
avalanche of energized sound. I've heard that litany hun-
dreds of times and every single time I've been aware of
the enormous power Aristide possessed in this capacity
to unify and articulate the deep feelings of those thousands of poor Haitian people who flocked to hear him
and who'd never had a champion before. Far too many
of his critics, ultra-suspicious (and not a little jealous) of
this gift of his, afraid of the apocalyptic potential of what
they dismissed as 'demagoguery', simply prophesied
doom and gloom.[6]

Aristide was, in fact, releasing new energy into Haiti's tired political and societal life. Of course, it might all turn out to be froth and these people just an ill-disciplined mob, but, with goodwill, and a commitment to harness this raw energy, it could also open a new chapter in Haiti's history. Aristide's critics watched him stir up the feelings of these poor people. Then they just waited for all the energy to dissipate and the promises to dissolve. It was easy just to blame him for his lack of political skills and for getting things all wrong. Yet their own lofty cynicism and hand-washing cowardice were arguably a far greater contributing factor to the eventual failure of Aristide's dream. They didn't even begin to understand what was happening around them. Aristide began to call this participation of the Haitian people in shaping their own future a 'second independence'. The first independence, that of 1804, was always considered a glorious birth but one accomplished without the aid of a midwife. The second might have been no less glorious. But this time the 'midwives' were waiting with buckets of cold water in which to drown the struggling new arrival before it drew its first breath.

And so it turned out. Pressure from the bishops led to his resignation from the priesthood. A military coup ousted him from office a mere seven months after taking power. He was able to fulfil only a fraction of his mandate and, like Duvalier, needed constantly to look over his shoulder for the next opponent he'd have to deal with. Four years after leaving the presidential office, he ran again and is currently serving a second term. During this time he will head the celebrations to mark Haiti's 200 years of independence. And he'll be running a political machine that's bankrupt of ideas, totally without energy, a failure judged by any standard.

Aristide is a democratically elected president in a state

that has no functioning legislature, no judiciary, no civil society, no organized political parties and no economy to speak of. Only the executive arm of government functions. When he acts, he has to do so by decree. That, of course, makes him a dictator even if he'd want to claim otherwise. He's been abandoned by his friends at home and abroad. The hope that surrounded his election in 1990 has totally disappeared. Once again, Haiti is an object of ridicule in the eyes of the world if, that is, anyone cares to spare a thought for it.

Liberation theologians seem to have no formula or methodology that can help poor Haiti in its present plight. Yet somebody ought to be applying the same rigorous analysis of the contextual factors affecting the political life of the nation, and some of those factors are external to Haiti. The desperate poverty of the people flows as much from the way the world conducts its business and the needs of Washington to keep everyone in their back yard in their proper place. It is surely scandalous that a 90-minute plane journey separates the wealthiest people on earth from some of the poorest.

A very special anniversary falls during the course of Lent 2003: 7 April marks the 200th anniversary of the death of Toussaint Louverture. Toussaint was born the son of a king of the Aradas tribe from Dahomey in West Africa. He was among the tens of thousands shipped into slavery in the New World. He was a deeply Christian man and clearly a natural leader. When the slaves of Haiti began their struggle for independence, they looked to him for inspiration. He commanded his rough-and-ready troops deploying them astutely and showing great personal courage. Napoleon referred to him dismissively as a 'gilded African'. Others, thinking of his prodigious horsemanship, described him as the 'centaur of the savannahs'. One of the French generals he did battle with admired him greatly. 'You never met Toussaint without fear,' he said, 'nor left him without emotion.' When he wrote to Napoleon he wrote 'to the first of the whites' but signed off as 'the first of the blacks'.

This simple man of faith, a family man who loved nothing more than working in his garden, led his people to the very brink of victory in their wars with the French. Having trusted a French official, he was tricked into captivity and shipped back to France. He was incarcerated in the dungeon of the Château de Joux in the Jura Alps. He wasted away in his cold and damp prison cell. His teeth rotted and he was covered with sores and died in misery. He'd written some defiant words to Napoleon. 'In overthrowing me,' he said, 'you have cut down in St Domingue only the trunk of the tree of liberty. It will spring up again from the roots for they are numerous and deep.' His life came to an end just nine months before Haiti declared its independence from France on 1 January 1804.

William Wordsworth penned one of his finest sonnets as a tribute to Toussaint. It was written shortly after the Haitian hero had been taken into captivity:

Toussaint, the most unhappy man of men!
Whether the whistling rustic tend his plough
Within thy hearing, or thy head be now
Pillowed in some deep dungeon's earless den; –
O miserable Chieftain! Where and when
Wilt thou find patience? Yet die not: do thou
Wear rather in thy bonds a cheerful brow:
Though fallen thyself, never to rise again,
Live, and take comfort. Thou hast left behind
Powers that will work for thee; air, earth, and skies;
There's not a breathing of the common wind
That will forget thee; thou hast great allies;

They friends are exultations, agonies,
And love, and man's unconquerable mind.

The story of Toussaint is the story of Haiti. Its finest people
and all its hopes and dreams have been squandered or plun-
dered down the ages.

I will end this chapter with a story that explains why I go
on believing that all is not lost as far as Haiti is concerned.
It's the tale of a woman whose name I cannot even remember. She was in church one Sunday morning when I arrived
to lead the service. I used to spend half an hour catching up
on people's news and establishing a liturgy that included
the various requests to participate, which I only discovered
on arrival. Eventually all was ready and we began. At one
point in the service, a woman came forward (as arranged)
to give her testimony. She told the congregation that, in the
course of the previous week, she'd had to bury one of her
children, an 18-month-old baby boy. I stopped her in order
to ask how many other women in church that morning had
had the same experience. Hands went up until I became
aware that every woman of childbearing age had known
the grief felt by this poor woman in front of us. She completed her sorry tale and then began to sing.

She'd chosen an old hymn that a missionary in former
years must have translated from English to Créole. We
no longer sing it these days, it's considered a little out of
fashion and inferior. That day, however, as this poor
peasant woman sang its words, it broke my heart and yet
lifted my spirit at the same time. She broke down in tears in
the chorus and we all joined in to help her finish it. This is
what she sang:

In loving kindness Jesus came
My soul in mercy to reclaim:

And from the depths of sin and shame,
Through grace, he lifted me.

*From sinking sands – he lifted me;*
*With tender hand – he lifted me;*
*From shades of night to plains of light,*
*O praise his name – he lifted me.*

It is the faith of that woman that keeps hope alive in my breast. François Duvalier came to power to address her needs and change her lot. He lost the plot. This woman was also the reason for Jean-Bertrand Aristide's drift into politics. But he too lost his way and proved that, whatever his gifts as a priest, he had no stomach for the fight to change her lot. It was this woman for whom Toussaint Louverture died, but for all his claim that the tree of liberty would go on replenishing itself even when the trunk had been cut down, 200 years of Haitian history tell a different tale. It was this woman for whom Christ died, and it's up to Christians everywhere, liberation theologians among them, to show that his death wasn't in vain.

———————————

## Questions for discussion

1. Has this chapter seemed too 'social or 'political' to be studied in Lent?

2. Do you believe that sin can be structural and institutional as well as personal?

3. How can hope survive in places like Haiti?

4. Is there a passage of scripture that comes to your mind as you think about the woman whose child died?

# Fractured identities: the post-colonial world

I went to study theology at Cambridge in the late 1960s. I already had a degree in English literature and was aware that Cambridge was home to two luminaries whose works I'd long greatly admired. Basil Willey was one, the King Edward VII Professor of English Literature, successor to Sir Arthur Quiller-Couch and author of a number of important books like, for example, *The Seventeenth Century Background*. He always described himself as more a historian of ideas than a master of literary criticism. His mind roamed the intersecting territories of literature, philosophy, history and theology. He'd had to establish himself within the Cambridge faculty at a time when his colleague F. R. Leavis was high priest for an approach to literary works that focused narrowly on the texts. Willey, who much preferred to look at literature within the context that had produced it, developed the English degree course at Cambridge under the general title: 'Literature, Life and Thought', specializing on the 'Life and Thought' parts himself. He often quoted a phrase of Sir Thomas Browne, one of his own seventeenth-century heroes, to describe himself. Browne claimed that he'd sought to live in 'divided and distinguished worlds', keeping a foot in each of the rapidly diverging camps of religion and science. Willey too, a contemporary of C. P. Snow whose *Two Cultures* had made a huge impact when it was delivered as the Rede Lecture in 1959, wanted an interdisciplinary approach to culture. He deemed it necessary to develop an educational system that allowed and encouraged young people to move between disciplines rather than get tied down by the tendency towards specialization then becoming so oppressively prevalent in our schools.

Then, at Jesus College (just over the wall from where I was living) was Raymond Williams whose *Culture and Society* had appeared in 1958 and who was offering a Marxist analysis of literature and society that was attracting a great deal of attention. In the event, it was a 'protégé' of Williams, a young research fellow named Terry Eagleton, who succeeded in drawing my own eye and firing my imagination. About my age, Eagleton was a Roman Catholic who launched the magazine *Slant* during my years at Cambridge. Here was a brilliant young academic attempting to hold together Marxism and Roman Catholicism in the spirit, as he understood it, of the recently concluded Vatican Council. It was audacious and I fell in love with it all. Eagleton later moved to Oxford and is now professor of cultural theory in Manchester. His writing has always been of great interest to me since those early days.

It was a book review written by Eagleton that drew my attention to a collection of essays by Homi Bhabha entitled *The Location of Culture*.[1] I was grabbed by the very first line of Eagleton's piece: 'Post-colonial theory', he wrote, 'is written on the hoof, a language of migration and displacement, of split locations and fractured identities.' I went out the very same day, bought the volume and devoured it. It is, indeed, as fine as its reviewer claimed. As I read, I found myself making an index of what seemed to me to be the key words in Bhabha's analysis, and the results were fascinating. The post-colonial world is fractured and fragmented all right. Our cities are wonderfully yet bewilderingly multi-ethnic. The London borough in which I live has over 100 different language groups living within its borders, all needing education, health care and social services. Bhabha urges us to beware of responding to multi-culturalism simply by admiring its exoticism, loving its food, its carnivals and its colour. Nor should we view the diversity of cultures around us with too dispassionate an eye, comparing and contrasting them while keeping them in hermetically sealed compartments. It's the *hybridity of culture* that matters to Bhabha, that's what needs to imprint itself on our minds and hearts. The challenge of post-colonial societies, according to his argument, should evoke a response beyond the merely aesthetic (or academic); it should rather create an awareness of how the various elements within a cultural matrix overlap, are interdependent, belong together. It's the idea of 'cross-over' that permeates Bhabha's book and the index I'd compiled turned out to be a veritable thesaurus of words and metaphors to illustrate this. Beyond, side-by-side, in-between, negotiation, the Third Space, hybridity, split, mimic man, displacement – all these words and phrases suggest in one way or another the fundamental mixed-upness of contemporary society.

Terry Eagleton's praise for Homi Bhabha has the practical aim of bringing an agenda of great importance to the awareness of the more general reader. 'Few post-colonial writers', Eagleton writes, 'can rival Homi Bhabha in his exhilarated sense of alternative possibilities – of a world in which "hybridity", "in-betweenness", a culture in permanent transition and incompleteness, may be embraced without anxiety or nostalgia. The very process of Bhabha's writing – intricate, thickly layered, veering from poetry to theory to rhetoric – enacts this dissolving of familiar co-ordinates.'

These are the very factors that have led to the emergence of a body of literature for which the only adequate descriptive tag would be 'world writing'. People such as Toni Morrison, Peter Carey and Ngugi wa Thiong'o are among the leading authors in this development. They write out of a close (or even direct) relationship with the experience of migration. Morrison is part of the Black diaspora that saw millions of Africans transported to the Americas in the era of slavery and she writes powerfully about it. Carey is part of a little less dramatic population transfer that saw large numbers of European people settle large areas around the world. And Ngugi, exiled from Kenya since the early 1980s, writes directly from an experience of displacement, a fate shared with millions of others who have had to leave their homelands for political or economic reasons.

Writers such as these explore global themes where it is precisely the dissolving of familiar co-ordinates that opens up a rich vein of human experience for consideration. Hybridization and cross-fertilization offer a template for much of this writing.

No one has wrestled longer or harder with these factors than Salman Rushdie. Writing in defence of *The Satanic Verses*, which had aroused such strong feelings when it appeared in 1988, he declared that the novel:

> celebrates hybridity, impurity, intermingling, the transformation that comes of new and unexpected combinations of human beings, cultures, ideas, politics, movies, songs. It rejoices in mongrelization and fears the absolutism of the Pure. *Mélange*, hotchpotch, a bit of this and bit of that is *how newness enters the world*. (sic) It is the great possibility that mass migration gives the world, and

I have tried to embrace it. *The Satanic Verses* is for change-by-fusion, change-by-conjoining. It is a love song to our mongrel selves.[2]

Rushdie's 1999 novel *The Ground Beneath Her Feet* develops this post-modern agenda still further. It tells the life story of two rock stars, Vina Apsara and Ormus Cama, and describes their love for one another and their near-deification during the 1970s and 1980s when, as the founders of a band called VTO, they became the most famous rock and roll act in the world. The tale is told by Umeed Merchant, a photographer who has loved Vina since they were both children.

The novel is saturated in Greek myth, steeped in allusions to Homer, Virgil and Ovid: the story of Vina and Ormus is in part the story of Orpheus and Eurydice; Ormus descends to a kind of hell and loses Vina at the end. Vina is in part Helen, over whom men start battles and in part Persephone, lured by her father's brother to the underworld. This is a novel that asks us to compare new myths and old ones and to test each for their groundedness. Greek myth mingles with the mythology of India and the whole is spiced by the easier mythology of contemporary celebrity.

The teller of the tale, the photographer, is a world-renowned master of an art that, as is stated from the outset, can both capture reality and falsify it. A photographer is someone who sits on the sidelines and observes life rather than participates in it. Umeed Merchant is indeed an outsider. His work places him on the outside but this position is further emphasized by the fact that he belongs to the Muslim branch of a Bombay family with impeccable Hindu credentials. The Hindu relatives, three generations later, still consider their Muslim kinsfolk to be apostate. As well as turning their back on their Hindu religious beliefs, we learn that Umeed Merchant's family have taken the further step of rejecting the Muslim faith too. They've become 'non-religious Muslims'. With all this in mind, it can hardly be surprising that 'outsideness' becomes a recurring theme that runs right through this kaleidoscopic novel.

This is given full play in the theories of Sir Darius Xerxes Cama, Vina's father. He holds that 'in every generation there are a few souls . . . who are simply *born not belonging* (sic), who come into the world undetached, if you like, without strong affiliation to family or location or race'.[3] They are pushed to the sidelines because, on the whole, the world is organized in favour of those who value stability and who fear transience and feel threatened by uncertainty and change. They erect 'a powerful system of stigmas and taboos against rootlessness, that disruptive, anti-social force, so that we mostly conform, we pretend to be motivated by loyalties and solidarities we do not really feel, we hide our secret identities beneath the false skins of those identities which bear the belongers' seal of approval'.[4] The truth lies deeper than that, of course. It's in our dreams and literature that we celebrate difference and honour those who have the courage to stand outside conventional expectation.

There are more such people than can be imagined. They long to be free. Invoking the metaphor of 'the road' that seems to crop up again and again through the pages of this little book, he spells out the dream of post-modern men and women. 'No sooner did we have ships than we rushed out to sea,' he writes, 'sailing across oceans in paper boats. No sooner did we have cars than we hit the road. No sooner did we have airplanes than we zoomed to the furthest corners of the globe. Now we yearn for the moon's dark side, the rocky plains of Mars, the rings of Saturn, the interstellar deeps . . . [It's got to the point where] we hunger for warp space, for the outlying rim of time. And this is the species that kids itself it likes to stay at home, to bind itself with – what are they called again? – *ties*.'⁵

This unquenchable thirst for new experience, the drive to keep exploring new frontiers, to celebrate 'outsideness', is a risky business. It takes people beyond the realm of recognizable landmarks; it's another example of Michel Foucault's 'limit experience'. For all the dangers, one can only become aware of one's own potential when living at (or even beyond) one's known limits. As Vina's celebrity increases so she is drawn into a globe-trotting life with all the demands that accompany such a life. There are gigs and long hours in recording studios, interviews and parties and photo opportunities. Her life becomes more and more a public commodity. And all of this is sometimes hard to sustain, especially for a self-made person who invented her own name and developed an identity for herself through sheer will power and an almost insatiable hunger for life. When it becomes too much for her, in a search for solace, she sometimes seeks the consolation of religion. But Umeed, the great observer, is never taken in. He has no time for systems of belief, which he dismisses as examples of 'unreliable narration'. To him, faith is irony, he puts his trust more in the creative imagination, in fictions that, not pretending to be fact, end up telling the truth. 'All religions have one thing in common,' he declares, 'namely that their answers to the great question of our origins are all quite simply wrong.'⁶

Umeed recognizes that from time to time he has recourse to the use of religious language but won't allow that to suggest the possibility of religious belief. He puts that down to a 'pre-religious' love of metaphor and the need some-times to express the inexpressible and to describe our dreams of otherness. But religion, to his mind, far from being a vehicle to help the imagination deal with such material, does the opposite. 'Religion came and imprisoned the angels in aspic,' he declares before adding, 'the god of the imagination is the imagination. The law of the imagination is whatever works. The law of the imagination is not universal truth, but the work's truth, fought for and won.'[7]

He is deeply suspicious of religion in general and monotheism in particular. Indeed he dismisses monotheism as just another despotism. To his mind, the only value of religion lies in its 'stories', but these can be enjoyed only when we stop believing in the gods they tell of. If, one day, we woke up to find that there were no more devout Christians, Muslims, Hindus, Jews on earth, then (and only then) could we enjoy the beauty of their stories because they wouldn't be dangerous any more. The only truth they'd now contend for would be that contained within the limits of the 'well-told tale'. Religion would have given way to literature.

This flight away from belief in stories that are held up to be 'true' and towards belief in those stories merely as fictions of the imagination seems to be a good description of Rushdie's own path and position. It moves the question of any response we might make from the realm of ethics to aesthetics, from the 'I ought' of a moral imperative to the 'I like that' stimulated by any work of the imagination.

Vina Apsara's religious consolations turn out to be consumer durables; they rarely last very long. Her lover, meanwhile, seems to resort to an altogether different resource. He clings to the 'vision of a literally disintegrating world held together, saved and redeemed, by the twin powers of music and love . . . I envied its off-the-wall coherence, its controlling overview.' The novel puts pop music forward as having real binding force for our postmodern world. It crosses over ethnic and other cultural differences and has a following in every continent of the globe. It's virtually become a universal language; it's certainly a vehicle that carries the messages of the day.

In the face of the horrors and breast-beating of the Vietnam war, music alone seems able to shape and carry an adequate response. 'In this dark time,' the narrator declares, 'it's the rock music that represents the country's most profound artistic engagement with the death of its children, not just the music of peace and psychotropic drugs but the music of rage and horror and despair . . . [There is] a humane democratic spirit-food fullness in its response.'[8] The importance of popular music is not limited to its angry outbursts. It also seems able to introduce a notion of love or peace into so much of the ugliness and strife of a world at war with itself. It has a unique capacity to cling to beauty and innocence in a time of death and guilt. It alone seems able to give people faced by destruction a continuing appetite for life. The Manic Street Preachers would have been happy with that. And pop music is presented as possessing the vitality and binding capacity previously to be found in faith and religion. They, it's claimed, are now defunct, empty, bankrupt. For the generations who belong to a globalized age, exposed to messages that have been set free from the particularities of local or even continental cultures, values and attitudes are formed instead by the skilfully packaged and commercially marketed messages that come from popular music. In terms of giving the world a sense of unity, the job done in the past by Latin and English, or by Christendom and Islam, is now increasingly falling on the shoulders of angry, often alienated, singing groups whose music can be heard throbbing from personal Walkmans on trains and planes, blaring from open car windows in a busy street, deafening the sardine-like hordes who throng in to the bewilderingly large number of nightclubs to be found in all our cities, or played on stack stereo sets in kids' bedrooms around the world.

These are cross-over times all right and there is undoubtedly something exhilarating about the freedom to move between sectors and groups that were previously sealed off from each other. But there are dangers too. When all the landmarks go, then people sometimes discover they are lost. In the search for new experience, wider horizons, further shores, people might just forget who they are or where they belong. *The Satanic Verses* begins by showing two characters falling on to an English beach from a hijacked plane from India that's been flying at the height of Mount Everest. Two passengers, who can easily be understood as two aspects of the same character, survive and live adventure-packed lives in England. The novel ends by reuniting these characters, in effect bringing both sides of a divided self back together again. It is in India, where the novel began, and where both these characters grew up, that the healing takes place. Only by going home is this wholeness rediscovered. All of which simply underlines the angst that often lurks below the apparently joyous, certainly surrealistic, fast-moving narrative of Rushdie. Just as Jack Kerouac was warned by William Burroughs about the dangers of self-delusion in looking to Buddhism for meaning, so one feels that Rushdie too deceives himself from time to time. His racy prose throws up a smokescreen behind which anxiety lurks.

A long passage in *The Ground Beneath Her Feet*, a passage that looks at rootlessness, outsideness and the nature of happiness, ends with a rather bleak statement: 'One must simply overcome, always overcome. Pain and loss are "normal" too. Heartbreak is what there is.' As the Latin poet Virgil put it: *Sunt lacrimae rerum* ('there are tears at the heart of things'), or as the pop singer Beck declared in one of his songs, 'All alone is all you are.' The cry is as old as time. And if religion is rejected, it is not always apparent where solace will come from.

Later in the book, quoting Euripedes this time (rather than Virgil), the message is equally bleak:

> May the gods save me from becoming a stateless refugee!
> Dragging out an intolerable life in desperate helplessness!
> That is the most pitiful of all griefs; death is better. [sic]

And that really does seem both to be the rock-bottom message of much of Rushdie's work and also his warning, intentional or not, to an age set upon enjoying hybridity, rootlessness, in-between-ness, the limit experience. Indeed, in the aftermath of the publication of *The Satanic Verses*, Salman Rushdie seemed himself the perfect embodiment of 'the stateless refugee' whose plight Euripedes pitied.

Many of the themes treated by Rushdie are also to be found in the writings of his protégé and friend Hanif Kureishi. Kureishi's father, from a relatively affluent Muslim family in Madras, came to Britain in 1947 to read law. Most of the rest of his family, meanwhile, moved to Pakistan after partition and Kureishi's father discontinued his studies in London to take up a clerical job in the embassy of this newly founded Pakistan, a country in which he had never set foot. He met and married an English woman from a lower middle-class background and they lived in Bromley. Hanif was born there in 1954, one of the first generation of children of 'New Commonwealth' origins born in Britain. All of which contributes to a feeling of 'outsideness', a theme he reflects on a great deal in his writing.

Kureishi grew up in the London suburbs and attended the same school as pop singer David Bowie. Bowie became an immensely successful singer and, unlike others in that business, maintained his position over a long period of time. Bowie was greatly influenced by a stepbrother who introduced him to the Beat poets and the music of the 1950s. He achieved his success largely by constant changes of image and identity, which allowed him to steer his way through the confusing 1970s. He spent time in a Buddhist monastery, appeared in drag, led the glam-rock movement, played on his ambiguous sexuality, went in for a bewildering array of fashion metamorphoses and led a number of avant-garde experiments in the rock industry.

Kureishi's 1995 novel *The Black Album* bore the same title as a record released commercially just a year earlier by pop singer Prince who was widely acknowledged to continue very much in Bowie's tradition. A description of the singer offered by one of the characters in the novel relates that 'He's half black and half white, half man, half woman, half size, feminine but macho too . . . He's a river of talent. He can play soul and funk and rock and rap'.[9] Like Bowie, Prince is the very model of modern adaptability and, once again, we see cross-over and hybridity, in-between-ness and negotiated space very much in evidence.

The natural place, in Kureishi's view, for the working out of these themes is the inner city. He was critical of a number of costume-drama television and film productions that, focusing very much on the 'heritage' aspects of England, were almost always set lavishly within some sweet especial rural scene. To his mind, these productions aimed at giving an impression of a national unity that was radically dissociated from the facts. He looked to the inner city, and especially to London, as settings for his themes. Here the culturally and demographically hybrid nature of the city represents a space where new, non-hierarchical and pluralistic kinds of individual and national identity that reflect the reality of modern Britain's increasing cultural diversity can potentially be forged. Indeed, within the inner city can be seen the 'microcosm of a larger British society struggling to find a sense of itself, even as it was undergoing radical change'.[10] In a commentary on 'Englishness' in the inter-war period Kureishi attempted to measure that struggle. He noted that J. B. Priestley had observed the existence of three Englands. First, there was the guidebook England of palaces and forests; then nineteenth-century industrial England with its factories and terraced streets; and finally, contemporary England with its bypasses and suburbs. 'Now,' he concludes, 'there is another England as well: the inner city.' This England is a much easier context within which diasporic populations can discover themselves. By claiming to be Londoners, black people can express a 'national' identity that respects their cultural differences when set against mainstream society.

So Kureishi, exploring cultural diversity within the inner-city areas of the London of his birth, writes 'world literature', novels and plays that address the themes of displacement and hybridity, without moving very far at all. The material for his works seems to spring naturally from his own life and experience.

*My Beautiful Laundrette*, one of Kureishi's earliest works, a film of rare and tender beauty, tells the tale of two boys who'd grown up together in London's East End. Johnny is Caucasian, Omar Pakistani. As children in school they're bosom pals before they get sucked into their own separate sub-cultures. Johnny becomes involved in National Front activities, shaves his head, joins demonstrations, becomes unemployed. Omar is soon drawn into the word of small business and is surrounded by uncles and cousins involved in drug-dealing. He is given his own business to run, a laundrette, and it is while on these premises that he recognizes his erstwhile friend Johnny marching in the street as part of a fascist demonstration. He makes contact again and invites Johnny to come and work for him. The renewal of their friendship leads to an awareness of love between them. This same-sex relationship, worked out against the odds and despite huge cultural obstacles, is held up as a thing of beauty against a backdrop of the eddying waters of racism, crime, drug-dealing and gangsterism so readily to be found in the inner city. It becomes a thing of beauty in its in-between-ness and hybridity, but something so tender that it might be snuffed out at any time.

Again and again, Kureishi paints pictures that reveal just how difficult it is both to forge an identity and also to find something solid to cling to in the shifting sands of the inner city. *Black Album* tells the story of Shahid Hasan, a student at an inner-London university who is being pulled in different directions by various forces competing for his commitment. The novel was written in 1989, the year when the Berlin wall came down and also the year when the Ayatollah issued his fatwah against Salman Rushdie. The ideologies behind both these events are strongly present on campus. A character named Brownlow is a communist party activist and another named Riaz gathers a group of radical fundamentalist Muslims around him. Shahid comes into contact with both and considers their claims carefully, but it is his relationship with Brownlow's partner Deedee Osgood that proves far more formative. She is one of his tutors and there are interesting discussions about the nature of the courses she teaches. She wants to move the study of English literature away from the acknowledged canon in the direction of a globalized 'cultural studies' course. He resists this; for him, 'serious reading required dedication. Who,' he wondered, 'now believed it did them good? And how many people knew a book as they knew *Blonde on Blonde*, *Annie Hall* or *Prince* even? Could literature connect a generation in the same way? Some exceptional students would read hard books, most wouldn't, and they weren't fools.'[11] For Shahid, Deedee's readiness to study anything that took her students' interest seemed a very 'post-modern' thing to do. Her willingness to consider anything from 'Madonna's hair to a history of the leather jacket', interesting as these things might be in a short-term sort of way, did seem to represent a subtle new form of exclusion rather than empowerment of the minorities on whose behalf she seemed so interested.

Despite these disagreements, however, Deedee and Shahid were soon in a passionate relationship in defiance of so many conventions. It was a student–teacher relationship that crossed racial boundaries and, within it, it was the white woman who proved to have the voracious sexual appetite when the stereotype might have supposed that to be the characteristic of the black male. Kureishi seems to want to take a pot-shot at as many prevailing conventions as he can.

In this mixed-up world of make-over and cross-over, Shahid found it difficult to find his place. He was at sixes and sevens. He 'was afraid his ignorance would place him in no man's land. These days everyone was insisting on their identity, coming out as a man, woman, gay, black, Jew – brandishing whichever features they could claim, as if without a tag they wouldn't be human. Shahid, too, wanted to belong to his people. But first he had to know them, their past and what they hoped for.'[12] He made serious attempts to learn as much as he could about the culture and spirituality of 'his people' and part of this effort was to seek to learn how to pray. In his attempts to do this, he:

> had little notion of what to think, of what the cerebral concomitant to the actions should be. So, on his knees, he

celebrated to himself the substantiality of the world, the fact of existence, the inexplicable phenomenon of life, art, humour and love itself – in murmured language, itself another sacred miracle. He accompanied this awe and wonder with suitable music, the 'Ode to Joy' from Beethoven's Ninth, for instance, which he hummed inaudibly.[13]

Kureishi is never as cynical or dismissive about religion as Rushdie as this imaginative and sensitive description of the meaning of prayer indicates.

Shahid and Deedee, after a tumultuous time together and many adventures, decide to try to make a go of their relationship. Shahid has thought hard about this and can cope with the idea by coming to terms with the necessity in the light of his experience to live in 'divided and distinguished worlds'. 'How could anyone confine themselves to one system and creed?' he asked. 'Why should they feel they had to? There was no fixed self; surely our several selves melted and mutated daily? There had to be innumerable ways of being in the world. He would spread himself out, in his work and in love, following his curiosity.'[14] And so, the story moves to its conclusion. The two of them take a train for Brighton where they intend to spend a weekend together. Once again, as with *My Beautiful Laundrette*, a loving relationship is held out as somehow offering a way to a meaningful and sustainable existence. But it is all so fragile. It will go on, 'until it stops being fun', Deedee says. Shahid agrees. And with that the novel ends.

Kureishi is an acute observer of suburban as well as inner-city life as his earlier novel, *The Buddha of Suburbia*, shows. The people who live on Acacia Avenue want spiritual experience tailored to their own needs. They don't, therefore, tend to expect anything from the churches or mosques with their predetermined and historically shaped liturgies but they turn rather to any peripatetic guru who'll come and offer his wares within their own front rooms. This is the essence of pick 'n' mix spirituality. The novel opens with an example of just such an occasion. The furniture in the front room is pushed back against the wall and middle-aged white people are sitting cross-legged on the floor. The lights are turned down and people encouraged to observe some simple rules of relaxation. After the yoga, there is talk of yin and yang, cosmic consciousness, Chinese philosophy and following the Way. Those sitting there become hypnotized by the smell of incense and the general atmospherics of the event.

Karim, the principal character in this novel, is the son of the guru (an Indian from Bombay married to a white English woman). Karim sets about observing his father's religious practices and this generates some interesting conversation between the two of them. 'We live in an age of doubt and uncertainty,' the father declares. 'The old religions under which people lived for 99 per cent of human history have decayed or are irrelevant. Our problem is secularism. We have replaced our spiritual values and wisdom with materialism. And now everyone is wandering around asking how to live. Sometimes desperate people even turn to me.' As he continues his discourse, he identifies happiness as the true object of life. 'I believe happiness is only possible,' he says, 'if you follow your feeling, your intuition, your real desires. Only unhappiness is gained by acting in accordance with duty, or obligation, or guilt, or the desire to please others. You must accept happiness when you can, not selfishly, but remembering you are part of the world, of others, not separate from them. Should people pursue their own happiness at the expense of others? Or should they be unhappy so others can be happy? There's no one who hasn't had to confront this problem.' This formula for life put forward by Karim's father is followed by a severe assessment of mainstream religion. 'So,' he avows, 'if you punish yourself through self-denial in the puritan way, in the English Christian way, there will only be resentment and unhappiness.'[15]

The narrative thus far has produced some powerful metaphors that centre on outside-ness, hybridity and cross-over. No Christian theologian in the period covered by this chapter can claim greater familiarity with these ideas than Hans Küng. The doctoral research undertaken by this Roman Catholic priest, his first major theological project, was a study of the doctrine of justification in the work of Karl Barth. The young scholar already had enough self-confidence to engage with a prototypical Protestant theologian and *the* archetypal Protestant doctrine.

Küng was a theological adviser at the Second Vatican Council and rejoiced in its readiness to embrace the spirit of the age. The apparent readiness of the Council to redefine authority in terms of the collegiality of the bishops instead of a heavily centralized papal office seemed so right to Küng. As did its openness to other Christians, other faiths and the modern world. The solid hegemony of a church unified by its Roman curia, a liturgy dating from the seventeenth century and the Latin language was also modified in favour of a vernacularized mass and more local expressions of popular piety. All this was food and drink for Küng. He was soon ready to write books for this new era of grace and they flowed from him over the years in a steady sequence. Some of them turned out to be too radical by far and, in 1979, after the publication of a book about the Church, his licence to teach was withdrawn to the great chagrin of many fellow Catholics and countless others too. Here was the 'stateless refugee' of Euripedes, the outsider par excellence.

But his industry intensified. In his attempts to deconstruct traditional ways of doing Christian theology, he offered dazzling critiques of a range of atheistic thinkers whose voices he urged his fellow believers to listen to with the greatest of care. His dialogue with artists, musicians, scientists, poets and novelists showed a similar eagerness to engage in open debate with thinkers of all kinds. This led him to the non-Christian faiths whose claims and teachings he continues to write about. His latest book, *Tracing the Way*,[16] accompanies a major television series shown in Germany and it outlines the 'spiritual dimensions of the World Religions'. His theses are startlingly radical. 'Salvation is possible for people outside the Roman Catholic Church,' he argues, 'and indeed outside Christianity. The question of truth and the question of salvation are not identical.'

Beyond these important books were others in which he set out some serious methodological considerations on how to identify and evaluate the factors present in 'paradigm shift'. He is convinced that we are living at a time when the paradigm of modernity is giving way to its successor paradigm and sets out to help his readers live through the bewildering changes of such a critical moment in time. This in turn leads him on to the question of a globalized culture with its concerns for ecology and human rights. He played a central part in the 1993 Parliament of World Religions as a result of which the Global Ethic Foundation (of which he is president) was set up. Increasingly, as he draws near the end of his productive life, he draws all his thinking together in the following mantra:

No peace among the nations without peace among the religions.

No peace among the religions without dialogue between
the religions.
No dialogue between the religions without global ethical
criteria.
No survival of our globe without a global ethic.

Küng has indeed lived in divided and distinguished worlds.
He has travelled to every corner of the globe, he has been
constantly 'on the road' in his search for authentic voices to
listen to. It's the *humanum* he's been interested in, the
human race, an entity beyond denomination, confession,
religion, race or culture. His work has been breathtaking in
its breadth and comprehensiveness and yet, upon analysis,
it's obvious that Küng has a clear sense of his identity. What
makes him, and all his fellow Christians, distinctive in their
search, is the person of Christ. And it's as the Christ-
centred pilgrim that he moves from one culture to another,
across religious boundaries, into other disciplines, from one
age (and one paradigm) to another. It is the map of his
Christology that continues to give him his sense of direction
was drawn as long ago as 1974 in his magisterial work, *On
Being a Christian.*

Küng always concentrates on the humanity of Jesus. It is
Christianity *as an historical faith* that has prevailed against
the mythologies, philosophies and mystery cults. It would
be better to be insulted as atheists than to lose sight of that
central fact. Jesus can be located and dated with some pre-
cision, but it's when Küng takes a good, hard look at the
New Testament evidence that he is particularly illuminat-
ing.

Jesus, he suggests, has often seemed to be 'domesticated'
within the churches, but he did not, in fact, belong to the
ecclesiastical and social establishment of his day. He had
nothing to do with the groups who wielded power, the high

(or chief) priest, the elders or the scribes. Jesus was not a priest, he was an ordinary layman. He was not a theologian. He was a villager and had certainly not been through a course of study. He put forward his own ideas directly and naturally and with amazing freedom. His interests were practical, he just wanted to advise and help people. He was not tied down to formulas and dogmas, he did not indulge in speculation or erudite legal casuistry. He was not a member or a sympathizer of the liberal-conservative government party. He was sustained by an intense expectation of the end. God's kingdom would come as grace, putting an end to suffering and death.

Galilee, the province where Jesus was born and raised, produced its fair share of revolutionary leaders (including the group known as the Zealots) who sought, by what would today be called guerilla resistance, to overthrow the Roman occupation of their homeland. Their activity fed a 'messianic expectation' for a leader who was to come. Jesus must certainly have fed a fair amount of speculation on this point. He preached radical change, attacked the ruling classes and the rich landowners. He spoke out against social abuses. He was certainly not the sweet, gentle, Jesus of later romanticism, nor the prudent diplomat, but, for all that, he did not indulge in polemics against Rome; he did not ask people to refuse to pay taxes or take part in a war of liberation; he did not stir up a class struggle. Instead, he was much more radical than the political activists of his day. He called people to love their enemies, to show unconditional forgiveness, to be ready to suffer rather than to destroy or retaliate or resort to the use of force or cultivate and nurse a sense of hate.

Nor did Jesus identify with those of his day who went down the road of apolitical radicalism, the Essenes, who by renunciation rather than rebellion sought to make their response to the turbulent times they were living through. Jesus was not an ascetic monk. He did not isolate himself mentally or physically from the world. His ministry took place in full view of the public. For him purity of heart was more important than ritualistic purity. He suffered no dualistic understanding of the world and reality, no split between the principles of light and darkness, good and evil. He was no ascetic, he defended his disciples who did not fast. He found sour-faced piety repulsive. He rejected ostentatious devotion. He seemed unable to see any over-riding importance in hierarchical order. For him, the lowest were to be the highest and the highest the servants of all. Subordination was to be reciprocal, expressed in models of mutual service.

Jesus also kept his distance from the other significant party of his day, the Pharisees. They were devout, right-eous, God-fearers who tried to keep the Law without offending the ethos of the day. Indeed, the survival of the Jewish people and culture after 70 AD was almost entirely due to them. But in the day of Jesus, they had become impossibly casuistical, hypocritical, in their judgemental-ism and in their attitudes towards the hellenizing Jerusalem establishment, to peasants and to tax-collectors. Unlike the Pharisees, Jesus recognized no taboos, he did not advocate an asceticism of fasting, he was not unbendingly scrupulous about sabbath observance. For him, what mattered was inward purity, correct attitudes of mind and a recognition that God's kingdom is God's work and not a human achievement. The Pharisees, to his way of thinking, were too concerned about externals.

So, Küng proceeds by rigorous analysis towards the conclusion that Jesus cannot be fitted in anywhere to the social scene of his day. He turns out to be provocative both to the left and to the right, challenging on all sides. He seems closer than the priests to God, freer than the ascetics in regard to the world, more moral than the moralists, more revolutionary than the revolutionaries. Moses was brought up at court, Buddha was a king's son, Confucius a scholar-politician, Mohammed a rich merchant. It really is amazing that Jesus, whose origins were so insignificant, should have continued to make his mark down the ages and across the continents.

It is worth asking, in view of the fact that over the course of this study we have seen a succession of people abandon Christianity for another (allegedly 'purer') religion, just what the Church has done with the person of Jesus to drive Jack Kerouac and Allen Ginsberg, George Harrison and the Beatles, Eldridge Cleaver and so many African-Americans, into the arms of Buddhism, Hinduism or Islam. Küng faces that question too.

He presents a startling scenario that shows just how the Church has 'shaped' Jesus for its various ends, rough hewn him according to its will. The 'Christ of Piety' shows Jesus as the pious, ever-friendly divine Saviour, the sweet Jesus of gentle and humble heart, the Jesus of Christmas carols 'the holy infant so tender and mild'. For some he is the divine Son of a much more human and loveable virgin mother. Artists have attempted in various ways to give their own images of Christ. What should we opt for?

Is it the beardless, young-looking, kind-hearted shepherd of the early Christian art of the catacombs; or is it the bearded emperor and ruler of the world in the image forms of the imperial cult of late antiquity; in courtly-rigid inviolability and menacing majesty before the gold background of eternity? Is it the *Beau-Dieu* of Chartres, or the German *Miserikordien-Helend* (man of sorrows)? Is it Christ the King and Judge of the world, enthroned on

the cross, on Romanesque portals and apses, or the cruel-
ly realistic suffering Christ in Dürer's *Christus im Elend*
and in the last Grünewald crucifixion still preserved?'[17]

There is great diversity in the Christ of popular piety, but
at least that Christ has a heart that beats and a face that
attracts. The 'Christ of Dogma' too often hides the humanity of Jesus behind complicated theological formulae. Even
the brilliance of the Chalcedonian definition, with its resolu-
tion of the christological problem in terms of the 'hypostatic
union', left the Church with a statement that proclaimed
that Christ 'is consubstantial with the Father, and with us
men, one person [a divine hypostasis] in whom are united
two natures – a divine and a human – without confusion or
change, without division or separation.' Hardly the stuff to
win the affection or admiration of the believer.

Even worse, from Küng's point of view, is the fact that
since all the early councils of the Church that wrestled with
this question were Greek, it's only too easy to recognize
behind the Christ image they formulated 'the unmoving,
passionless, countenance of Plato's God who cannot suffer,
embellished with some features of Stoic ethics'. And Küng
protests that Christ was not born in Greece. Daringly, he
goes on to suggest that the two natures doctrine is to some
extent at odds with the New Testament, that it did not solve
all the problems it addressed even in its own day, and
that in our day it is no longer comprehensible. Küng urges
theologians to give us less of a Christology in the classical
manner 'from above', and more of an historical Christology 'from below'. He wants us to have done with the
notion of 'Christ lodged in a very fine church, hospitalized,
domesticated', and a greater readiness to meet Christ in
ordinary life where neither dust nor too much gold is likely
to cover him up.

Such a move will, of course, create its own difficulties. There is another popular response to Jesus, one with a long history, that has given us the 'Christ of the Enthusiasts' – spirituals, flagellants, apostolic brethren, anabaptists, radical priests, independents, revivalists, charismatics, lone wolves, clowns, freaks . . . and . . . St Francis of Assissi! What Küng calls 'the Jesus movements' are frequently a protest against a domesticated plaster Christ in the churches who neither feels, nor can feel, pain. They are often part of more general protest against society, dull work, authority, boredom. Indeed, they can show great similarities of motivation with so many of the alienated voices we've been listening to throughout this little book. Neither a bourgeois ideology of progress nor a superficially revolutionary criticism of society, neither prosperity nor drugs nor humanisms can satisfy the (mainly) young people who follow Jesus in this way. For them, 'Jesus is, and becomes, constantly freshly relevant, apparently as fascinating as ever.' Küng mentions George Harrison's 'My sweet Lord, I really want to know you' and also a couple of stanzas from the musical *Hair*. It's very significant that the churches were busy criticizing this production because it showed people naked on stage. They should have been addressing the questions being put so hauntingly and insistently in these verses:

Where do I go?
Follow the river.
Where do I go?
Follow the gulls.
Where is the something,
Where is the someone
That tells me why
I live and die?

Follow my heartbeat.
Where do I go?
Follow my hand.
Where will they lead me?
And will I ever
discover why
I live and die,
I live and die?

Küng recognizes that much of the response of these enthusiasts is kitsch, showbiz stuff produced often enough under the influence of the narcotics industry. Nevertheless, he argues that:

> anyone who says that this sort of thing is a sacreligious distortion of the story of Jesus might well reflect how often in the past excessive piety has trivialized it. Critics who claim that only Jesus' humanity is portrayed here should remember how frequently his divinity alone was brought out in the churches. The complaint that the resurrection is left out of these presentations may be countered by pointing out how often theologies treated the crucifixion as no more than an unfortunate incident between the incarnation and the resurrection.[18]

Küng adds a short section on the 'Christ of Literature'. He shows how there has been a variety of literary forms used to explore the identity and claims of Jesus: short stories, poetry, novels, short prose pieces. Also literary techniques and themes and motifs: the returning Jesus, the defender of human freedom, the brother and friend of the poor and the oppressed, a resistance fighter, a social revolutionary, the model of all fools, clowns, lunatics, sufferers with AIDS, gay men, and the God-obsessed. The world of literature has often been more sensitive and perceptive to the person of Christ than the world of theology.

It is by working hard at keeping our picture of this vibrant, challenging Jesus that Christians have the best chance of continuing to speak with passion and conviction to the contemporary world. This is the distinctive mark of Christians and this is what they have to offer a fragmented world. The Jesus of the New Testament, 'provocative on all sides', can still speak to the displaced, the outsiders, the migrants, the young. In him we can still find a way to engage with an alienated, fractured society. Since he refused to be pinned down either within an identifiable sector of his contemporary world or within the categories or formulae of philosophers, theologians or politicians, he continues to offer a rallying point for those who live with hybridity and change, those who seek to live life to its limits. Hans Küng has wandered far and wide in his search for wisdom. He's been on the road. His writing and teaching seem to challenge a smug, defensive, insecure, obscurantist, authoritarian Church towards much more flexible and open positions.

It is over ten years since Archbishop George Carey, making a speech to a Swanwick Conference on *Gospel and Culture*, referred to a church he'd seen in Papua New Guinea that had no doors and no walls. People were able to come in or stay on the edges, listen for a while if they wished, and then walk away. 'I want an open church,' the archbishop pleaded, 'which is not afraid to be in the world.' Then he continued:

> My one abiding fear . . . is that the Church should settle for easy answers which will satisfy only those already convinced that Christ is the truth and that it may encourage the forces in our Church which actually wish to erect fences of doctrine and discipline leading to a sectarian fellowship of believers. I resist that because I believe with all my heart that the Church of Jesus Christ should be a Church of blurred edges, a Church of no walls, where people can ask their hardest questions without condemnation, and share their deepest fears without reproach . . . Too often we hear moralistic or experiential sermons which have no epistemological basis. I raise the question: will the gospel ever be public truth if our preachers are

not grappling with the challenge of scientism (sic) from their pulpits, or drawing on literature, art, science and theology to show that the Christian world view is relevant today?[19]

Blurred edges, no walls, open, engaged in the search for truth with people of other disciplines and faiths, pilgrims together on the road to greater understanding and deeper knowledge.

_____

## Questions for discussion

1. How do you view the presence in previously 'settled' communities of people from different cultural or ethnic backgrounds? Or, indeed, people with different lifestyles? Does it feel threatening? liberating? interesting or what? Has it changed any of the ways in which you act or think?

2. Do you agree with Hans Küng that there can be no peace among the religions and, indeed, no future for the world without dialogue between the religions? What opportunities for such dialogue do you have where you live?

3. Would you agree with Küng that it is Christ who gives Christians their unique identity and helps us define ourselves in a world of cross-over, hybridity and mixed-upness?

4. How do we focus the thinking and actions of the Church on Jesus again instead of its structures or its laws or its tradition? How can he be presented freshly and engagingly and challengingly to the world again?

# Afterword

I have already admitted the eclectic nature of this little book. And I quite see what superhuman efforts of the imagination and good faith you'll have made before arriving at this point. I'm sure that, as you worked your way through these pages, you must occasionally have dreamed of a very different kind of devotional book you'd have preferred to engage with. Perhaps you've had no difficulty agreeing with my basic approach but have torn your hair out at the voices I've chosen to listen to in the course of this narrative. You'd have chosen a quite different 'cast list' though in all likelihood yours would have begged just as many questions as mine.

What I hope is not in dispute is the seriousness of the task facing Christian theologians in these bewildering times. As I began to wrestle with some of the issues I've tried to deal with above, I knew I'd need help. I remember many a long conversation with Stuart Owen, for example, a young man who went on to become an Anglican priest. He helped me to tune my insensitive ears to a number of the issues that matter most to younger people. He accompanied me to a number of meetings where, very timidly, I tried out some of my rough and ready thoughts on unsuspecting audiences. Journeys home were lively affairs as Stuart offered his own reflections, some of them very frank, on my efforts. I owe him a great deal and am glad to acknowledge my debt here.

I have been preoccupied with some of these themes for a number of years and I've aired and shared them before a wide variety of audiences – a conference of school chaplains, for example, or a seminar at the Greenbelt festival, or a gathering of church leaders in the north of England, or a series of lunchtime talks in Winchester. They all produced much lively discussion and helped me work harder not only at the material I was presenting but also at the most helpful way to communicate such ideas to people not accustomed to thinking in this area. I'm convinced that we Christians have lost touch with much that's happening in the world around us. The Church is too often a place whose agenda seems barely relevant to the ordinary, everyday lives of the community it serves. We need to listen much harder to the voices coming to us from difficult places even when those voices seem to give expression to values and lifestyles we have little sympathy with. One of the hopes I have for this little book is that it might serve as a hearing aid for that act of listening. And, who knows, it might even persuade a few people that there's more of interest in an apparently hostile and secular culture than they ever thought possible.

That is a process I have gone through myself over the last few years. When a Canadian friend, Peter Goheen, sent me a copy of Eldridge Cleaver's *Soul on Ice*, I read it out of deference to him. He'd sent it out of the blue but, once I'd completed it, I knew I had to find room for it in my narrative. It was 30 years since I'd first read the book and, back then, I'd hated it. It wasn't much easier this time round but now I thought I heard a different note. The patent and cruel honesty of Cleaver's self-analysis, together with the clarity of his writing, seemed to give me access to the way African-Americans understand so much of the experience that has shaped their destiny and outlook on life. Any writer who can present such complicated and visceral material so that people shaped within radically different cultural matrixes can begin to understand what's happening speaks with a voice that should not be ignored.

The 'Science and Religion' agenda has been well-established for a long time now. The interfaith dialogue is also firmly fixed and is yielding a rich crop of seminars, symposiums and seminal writings. I want to offer my five pennyworth towards a conversation between modern culture and Christian theology in the belief that, in this area too, encounter and engagement need desperately to be cultivated. This little book is certainly no more than a discussion starter; but I'd love to think it might contribute to an intergenerational dialogue that is so much needed.

In a recent book, *Postmodernist Culture*,[1] Steven Connor describes the place of rock music in the contemporary world. '[It] has a claim', he writes, 'to be the most representative of postmodern cultural forms. For one thing, it embodies to perfection the central paradox of contemporary mass culture, in the fact of its unifying global reach and influence on the one hand combined with its tolerance and engendering of pluralities of styles, media and ethnic identities on the other.' A little later in his narrative, he makes a strong case for rock music's 'capacity to articulate alternative or plural cultural identities, of groups belonging to the margins of national or dominant cultures'.

Popular music is the component that runs through the pages of my narrative like the word 'Blackpool' through a stick of seaside rock. It's there in just about every chapter, insistently and unavoidably. Any consideration of the globalized nature of our contemporary culture must move beyond the worlds of finance and technology and deal also with the pervasive influence of pop music and pop videos. These media carry some of the most important and determinative messages of our era. They cannot be ignored.

I must convey one other word of thanks, this time to Maya Angelou. She has been a good friend for almost fifteen years now. She and her publishers (Virago Press) have allowed me to use an excerpt from her well-known poem *The Caged Bird* and I'm delighted to acknowledge my debt to them all for this gracious gesture.

So I offer this study in the full awareness of how provisional it will turn out to be. Its mistakes are all mine, of course, but my indebtedness to the goodwill and patience of others is patent. Let me end with some words from my friend Stuart Owen from a letter he wrote to me a few years ago. He described the rock 'n' roll scene and then asked a question: 'Where is the Church in all this? I think our guides have to be the parable of the prodigal son and Jesus' anointing at Bethany. Like the prodigal's father, we have to be out on the doorstep looking for signs of our child's return, not waiting inside for his arrival. Maybe, just maybe, if the prodigal had had to walk right up to his old home and knock on the door he'd have lost his nerve and gone back to die among the swine – but, as the story has it, he didn't have to make it that far on his own.'

Not only do we have to be out on the steps waiting, we have to have the same grace and compassion Christ showed at Bethany to recognize and accept the sincerity of our child's approach no matter how fumbled, botched and misguided it may appear on the surface.

And it's in that spirit that I leave this little book with you, however fumbled, botched and misguided it may appear on the surface. May it succeed in stimulating your thinking and, in some small measure, glorify God.

# Notes

## Chapter 1

1. James Miller, Review of *The Passion of Michel Foucault*, Harper Collins 1993 in *The Guardian*, 5 June 1993.
2. Steve Turner, *Jack Kerouac: Angel Headed Hipster*, Bloomsbury 1996, pp. 75–6.
3. Ann Charters, introduction to Jack Kerouac, *On the Road*, Penguin 1991, p. ix.
4. Charters, introduction to *On the Road*, p. xxi.
5. Jack Kerouac, *On the Road*, Penguin 1991, p. 10.
6. Kerouac, *On the Road*, pp. 128–9.
7. Kerouac, *On the Road*, pp. 197–9.
8. Allen Ginsberg, *Allen Ginsberg: Selected Poems 1947–95*, Penguin 1996, p. 49.
9. Ginsberg, *Allen Ginsberg: Selected Poems 1947–95*, p. 54.
10. Ginsberg, *Allen Ginsberg: Selected Poems 1947–95*, p. 55.
11. James Campbell, *The Beat Generation*, Secker and Warburg 1999, p. 154.
12. Campbell, *Beat Generation*, p. 171.
13. Turner, *Jack Kerouac*, p. 174, italics in the original.
14. Dietrich Bonhoeffer, *The Cost of Discipleship*, SCM Press 1966, p. 95.
15. Bonhoeffer, *Cost of Discipleship*, p. 97.
16. Bonhoeffer, *Cost of Discipleship*, p. 98.
17. Bonhoeffer, *Cost of Discipleship*, p. 35.
18. Bonhoeffer, *Cost of Discipleship*, p. 37.
19. Bonhoeffer, *Cost of Discipleship*, p. 13; 'Memoir' by G. Leibholz.
20. Dietrich Bonhoeffer, *Letters and Papers from Prison*, SCM Press 1971, p. 349.

21. Bonhoeffer, *Letters and Papers from Prison*, pp. 280–1.
22. Bonhoeffer, *Letters and Papers from Prison*, pp. 360.

## Chapter 2

1. Sheila Rowbotham, *Promise of a Dream*, Allen Lane/Penguin 2001, p. 144.
2. Jane Daggett Dillenberger, *The Religious Art of Andy Warhol*, Continuum 1998, p. 30.
3. Dillenberger, *Religious Art of Andy Warhol*, p. 13.
4. Dillenberger, *Religious Art of Andy Warhol*, p. 92.
5. Alan Clayson, *George Harrison*, Sanctuary Press 2001, pp. 186–7.
6. Clayson, *George Harrison*, p. 207.
7. Clayson, *George Harrison*, p. 208.
8. Clayson, *George Harrison*, p. 294.
9. Clayson, *George Harrison*, p. 319.
10. Clayson, *George Harrison*, p. 319.
11. Eldridge Cleaver, *Soul on Ice*, McGraw-Hill 1967, p. 194.
12. Cleaver, *Soul on Ice*, p. 195.
13. Cleaver, *Soul on Ice*, p. 11.
14. Cleaver, *Soul on Ice*, p. 15.
15. Cleaver, *Soul on Ice*, pp. 16–17.
16. Cleaver, *Soul on Ice*, pp. 34–5.
17. Cleaver, *Soul on Ice*, p. 56.
18. Cleaver, *Soul on Ice*, pp. 67–8.
19. Cleaver, *Soul on Ice*, p. 81.
20. *The Autobiography of Martin Luther King Jr*, edited by Clayborne Carson, Little Brown and Company 1999, p. 323.
21. *Autobiography of Martin Luther King Jr*, references in this section are from Chapter 18, pp. 187–205.
22. Maya Angelou, *The Heart of a Woman*, Virago 1997, pp. 172–3.
23. Angelou, 'The Caged Bird', *And Still I Rise*, Virago 1992, p. 72

## Chapter 3

1. Kenneth O. Morgan, *Rebirth of a Nation*, Oxford Paperbacks 1982, p. 352.
2. Richard Llewellyn, *How Green Was My Valley*, New English Library 1975, p. 87.

3. Mick Middles, *Manic Street Preachers*, Omnibus Press 1999, p. 43
4. Middles, *Manic Street Preachers*, pp. 31–2.
5. Niall Griffiths, *Grits*, Vintage 2001, p. 323.
6. Griffiths, *Grits*, p. 409.
7. Justine Jordan, *The Guardian*, 3 February 2001.
8. This account sums up a passage in Niall Griffiths, *Sheepshagger*, Jonathan Cape 2001, pp. 119–25.

## Chapter 4

1. Bernard Diederich and Al Burt, *Papa Doc: Haiti and its Dictator*, Bodley Head 1969.
2. Melville J. Herskovits, *Life in a Haitian Valley*, Knopf 1937.
3. James G. Leyburn, *The Haitian People*, Yale 1941.
4. Jean Price-Mars, *Ainsi Parla l'Oncle*, Port-au-Prince 1927.
5. These are extracts from a message given on Radio Haiti-Inter in November 1988. They appear in Jean-Bartrand Aristide, *In the Parish of the Poor*, Orbis 1991, pp. 101–7.
6. Leslie Griffiths, *The Aristide Factor*, Lion Press 1994, p. 140.

## Chapter 5

1. Homi Bhabha, *The Location of Culture*, Routledge 1994.
2. Salman Rushdie, *Imaginary Homelands*, Granta Books 1992, p. 394.
3. Salman Rushdie, *The Ground Beneath Her Feet*, Jonathan Cape 1999, p. 72.
4. Rushdie, *Ground Beneath Her Feet*, p. 72.
5. Rushdie, *Ground Beneath Her Feet*, p. 73.
6. Rushdie, *Ground Beneath Her Feet*, p. 123.
7. Rushdie, *Ground Beneath Her Feet*, p. 447.
8. Rushdie, *Ground Beneath Her Feet*, p. 265.
9. Hanif Kureishi, *The Black Album*, Faber and Faber 1995, p. 25.
10. Bart Moore-Gilbert, *Hanif Kureishi*, Manchester University Press 2001, p. 83.
11. Kureishi, *The Black Album*, p. 111.
12. Kureishi, *The Black Album*, p. 92.
13. Kureishi, *The Black Album*, p. 92.
14. Kureishi, *The Black Album*, p. 274.

15. Hanif Kureishi, *Buddha of Suburbia*, Faber and Faber 1990, p. 76.
16. Hans Küng, *Tracing the Way*, Continuum 2002.
17. Hans Küng, *On Being a Christian*, Fount 1977, p. 128.
18. Küng, *On Being a Christian*, p. 138.
19. These words uttered at the Swanwick Conference referred to in the text were reported in the *Church Times*, 24 July 1992.

## Afterword

1. Steven Connor, *Postmodernist Culture*, Blackwell 1997, 2nd ed., quotations are to be found on p. 207.